Praise for

People say "Jesus saves, ___ not actually do her ___
depth of its meaning. Josh McNall takes the powe. ___
the theological meaning of the atonement not only in
an intellectual pursuit but also to the depths of one's
soul. The reader is taken to new freedoms in his or her
personal life as a result of the healing presence of the
atonement. Using down-to-earth illustrations of conver-
sations with his children, as well as engaging in stories
from Medieval times, McNall weaves together the transforming power of "Jesus saves." Each chapter presents
personal exercises for the reader and group to truly
engage the text—to get it into daily living and thinking.

—Jo Anne Lyon
general superintendent emerita
the Wesleyan Church

Josh McNall isn't just an academic who can bestow his
knowledge to us. He is a teacher in the true sense of
the word. And an excellent writer. *How Jesus Saves* is a
question that is not left merely for the classroom, nor
can it be reduced to oversimplified evangelical slogans.
Everyone must wrestle with this question and its implications. McNall doesn't shy away from the objections
and tough questions surrounding what happened on a
Roman cross more than two thousand years ago when
Jesus died and rose again. What is it that we need and
how does God give that to us? This will be a go-to book
to communicate to ordinary people the multifaceted
ways that Jesus brings salvation to all who believe.

—Aimee Byrd
author of *The Sexual Reformation* and
Recovering from Biblical Manhood and Womanhood

McNall has written an engaging introduction to important questions about the work of Christ on our behalf. This is a wonderful resource for the church with clear explanations brought to life through consistent cultural references.

—Madison N. Pierce
associate professor of New Testament
Western Theological Seminary

For two millennia, Christians have wrestled with the question: How does Jesus save us? This question is no doubt complicated and has led to polarized debates, accusations of heresy, and myriad theories. Joshua McNall cuts through the noise by offering an answer that incorporates the depth and breadth of Scripture's teaching on Jesus's atonement for our sins. In doing so, readers are able to better understand the multifaceted beauty of God's love for us through Jesus's life, death, burial, resurrection, and ascension.

—Brandon D. Smith
assistant professor of theology and New Testament
Cedarville University
co-founder of the Center for Baptist Renewal

Josh McNall has done it again! Of all topics he could have covered in this book, the atonement is one of the toughest. And yet Dr. McNall has a gift of making tough topics so much more accessible. Even as a pastor of twenty-plus years, there were simply things in this book I needed to hear. Thanks for this great resource!

—Phill Tague
lead pastor
Ransom Church

We live in a world of mouths that seeks to create our own pathways to eternal salvation and righteousness. Despite of all this, the fact remains, Jesus Christ alone can save. We cannot save ourselves no matter what we attempt or how hard we try. We need the atoning work of Jesus on the cross of calvary to have the opportunity to be forgiven and obtain eternal communion with God in heaven. Dr. Josh McNall brilliantly walks through the various doctrinal understandings of the atonement in a way that is practical and applicable to any audience in this work. Put aside the distractions related to saving yourself and learn from a book that proclaims the fullness of God's greatest gift of reconciliation— *How Jesus Saves!*

—Dr. Jim Dunn
president
Oklahoma Wesleyan University

The power of language isn't only in what it makes us feel, but also in how it helps us live the days we are given. McNall successfully provides enough explanation and captivating creativity to help us understand the gravity of what Jesus has done. This book is soaked in potential. Read it and allow the detail that Jesus loves you to move from your head to your heart.

—David Kinnan
author and pastor
Fountain Springs Church

I'm so grateful for a book that helps Christians go beyond simply singing "Jesus saves" with gusto and fervor, and offers a framework to grasp *how* and *why* Jesus saves. McNall takes one of the greatest theological complexities and gives us simple and memorable handholds to understand Jesus's salvific work on the cross without losing the mystery of it all. *How Jesus Saves* points us back to a moment in human history when God's love was poured out for everyone, and points us forward toward deeper holiness and a fresh spiritual awakening.

—Andrea Summers
campus pastor/dean of spiritual formation
Indiana Wesleyan University

HOW
JESUS SAVES

HOW
JESUS SAVES

ATONEMENT FOR ORDINARY PEOPLE

JOSHUA M. MᶜNALL

 Seedbed

 ZONDERVAN REFLECTIVE

Seedbed Publishing, published in partnership with Zondervan Reflective

Requests for information should be addressed to:
Seedbed Publishing, *415 Bridge Street, Franklin, Tennessee 37064*
Zondervan, *3900 Sparks Dr. SE, Grand Rapids, Michigan 49546*

Zondervan titles may be purchased in bulk for educational, business, fundraising, or sales promotional use. For information, please email SpecialMarkets@Zondervan.com.

McNall, Joshua M., 1982-
   How Jesus saves : atonement for ordinary people / Joshua M. McNall. – Franklin, Tennessee : Seedbed Publishing ; Grand Rapids, Michigan : Zondervan Reflective, ©2023.

      pages ; cm. + 1 video disc

      ISBN: 9781628240412 (paperback)
      ISBN: 9781628241983 (DVD)
      ISBN: 9780310154662 (epub)
      ISBN: 9780310154679 (audio)
      OCLC: 1344158039

      1. Atonement. 2. Salvation--Christianity.   I. Title.

BT265.3.M36 2023   232.3   2022946517

Cover illustration and design: Nate Farro
Art direction: Nick Perreault
Interior design: PerfecType, Nashville, Tennessee

Printed in the United States of America

22 23 24 25 26 LBC 5 4 3 2 1

For Ewan Gregory,
king

Contents

Introduction

Atonement for Ordinary People

Daddy, how does Jesus save us by *dying* on the cross?" That was my young daughter's question as we lay upon her bunk after nightly prayer. If you're a parent, you know bedtime brings the deep questions. Prior favorites in our house include: "Daddy, why are you going bald?" and "Daddy, why do you groan when you get off the couch?" Some questions are delay tactics, like the fourteen glasses of water required for a child to be adequately hydrated for sleep. And some questions come seemingly from nowhere. But I knew where this question had come from. We had attended a funeral.

My daughter's uncle (Daniel) died when he was only thirty. That's almost the same age as Jesus. Daniel was the husband of my youngest sister. He was a pastor. And he succumbed to a terrible disease called ALS. My daughter knew that an early death was not "good news." So why was Jesus different? After all, we don't celebrate state-sponsored executions as a means of saving grace, especially if the victim is innocent. Why do Christians look to the cross specifically as our greatest symbol of hope? It's a good question.

Looking back on the bedtime conversation, I should have had a snappy answer. After all, I had just written a long book on the atonement—the branch of theology that speaks to the reconciliation ("at-one-ment") between God and humans because of what Jesus did.[1] That book had more than a thousand footnotes and was generally well-received amongst scholars. Which is to say, you've never read it. Academic texts don't normally make best-seller lists. And though it was dedicated to the very daughter who had asked the bedtime question, I knew my treatment of high-flying terms like "Irenaean recapitulation" and "penal substitutionary objections" would not help her. They might not help you either.

Those ideas matter—a lot, actually—but they need to be made more accessible.

That's the reason for the book you're holding now: we need a work on the atonement for ordinary people, not just theologians. If you want to go deeper on a particular question of history or interpretation, you may find it helpful to consult my longer text, *The Mosaic of Atonement: An Integrated Approach to Christ's Work*. Cross questions are not just for pastors and academics. The cross is for fishermen and fork-lift operators. It's for porn stars and prodigals, elder brothers and overachievers. The cross is for everyone, including children as they lie upon their beds. The biblical writers knew this: "My dear children, I write this to you so that you will not sin. But if anybody does sin, we have an advocate with the Father—Jesus Christ, the Righteous One. He is the atoning sacrifice for our sins, and not only for ours but also for the sins of the whole world" (1 John 2:1–2).

But how exactly does that work?

While "Jesus saves" is perhaps the most basic claim of Christianity, the ensuing question—*How?*—demands attention. This whole book resides within that single word. How does Jesus save us by the cross?

One answer to my daughter's question is, of course, that Jesus didn't stay dead. His death, we might say, didn't *stick*. But resurrection alone doesn't answer a question about salvation and the cross. After all, if Elvis or Tupac were raised from the dead, we might correctly say that the world was a very strange place. But we would not conclude that the occurrence offered salvation to all who believed.[2] Christ's resurrection is essential for atonement.[3] But it does not necessarily reveal why Scripture connects the gospel so frequently to what happened on a Roman cross. Despite my academic work, my first attempt to simplify the matter left me trotting out some Sunday school answers. Allow me to rehearse a few of them.

Cross Questions

"Well, honey, Jesus died for our sins." That's true. But the answer raises other questions. For instance, how can an innocent person justly die for the sins of the guilty? Don't the basic rules of justice prohibit that? If this happened in our legal system, as it sadly has, we would not celebrate it. The book of Proverbs says it this way: "Acquitting the guilty and condemning the innocent—the LORD detests them both" (17:15). How could Jesus justly take our penalty since he did not commit the crime? Are sins like frequent flier miles that can be exchanged by some cosmic transfer? And why would the death of Jesus for *our* sins make God reconciled with sinners, especially since it was human sin that caused Christ's suffering?

The cross also raises questions about forgiveness. For instance, couldn't God simply forgive humanity apart from Jesus's bloody death, especially if we expressed repentance for our sins? After all, isn't the meaning of forgiveness to *set aside* a debt without requiring payment? If Jesus "paid it all" (as one song proclaims), then what did God forgive? When my own children sin against me, I do not make their place in the family contingent upon the slaughter of an innocent sibling or the family pet. What does it mean to revel in the fact that our forgiveness is connected to Christ's "atoning sacrifice" for the sins of the whole world (1 John 2:2)?

If that weren't enough, Satan also barges in to the atonement conversation—like an annoying dinner guest, in red tights. The book of 1 John claims: "The reason the Son of God appeared was to destroy the devil's work" (3:8). But how often do you bring up Lucifer in public conversation? To strike up talk of the demonic at a sophisticated dinner party might get you labeled a nut in certain circles. And if the Son of God came to destroy the devil's work, why does it seem that Satan's work is still alive and well? Have you seen social media lately?

Another claim about the cross and resurrection is that it marks Christ's *triumph* over death. The empty tomb is proof of this accomplishment. Yet if Jesus really conquered death, why does death's reign seem so uncontested? As we survey human history, the grave seems like a heavyweight champion who may have been knocked down on Easter Sunday but came back as strong as ever. The mortality rate still hovers around 100 percent, however much we delay it with medicines, super foods, and exercise routines. If it is by Jesus's "wounds we are healed" (Isa. 53:5; 1 Peter 2:24), why had my sister's husband died and left her a young widow? Where is the evidence of Christ's triumph over death?

A final understanding of the cross sees it as a loving example to be imitated. "This is love," proclaims 1 John when speaking of Christ's death (4:10). And even earlier, Jesus called his followers to take up their own crosses in order to follow him (Matt. 16:24). Cross-bearing is a command for Christians. And the call to sacrificial love goes far beyond a literal crucifixion. "Do not resist an evil person." Jesus says, "If anyone slaps you on the right cheek, turn to them the other cheek also" (Matt. 5:39). These are hard statements. And some who work closely with the victims of abuse question whether the understanding of the cross as an example to follow actually enables and prolongs abuse as victims "follow Jesus" in refusing to resist the violence done against them. Is this true? Do some views of the cross perpetuate injustice?

Distraction: The Biggest Challenge to Atonement Doctrine

None of these questions arose specifically in my daughter's bedtime conversation. In fact, I had only begun to explain the matter when she got distracted and changed the subject to what was going on at school, the next day's schedule, and the Harry Potter book she was reading.

In our own ways, adults do that too.

Perhaps the biggest barrier to grasping Jesus's saving work is not a rational objection about non-transferable penalties or the meaning of forgiveness. Our biggest problem is distraction. In a digital age especially, our attention is repeatedly diverted by a flood of flashing, dinging, ringing, vibrating notifications (even as you try to read this short introduction). Interruptions—both trivial and important—assault us. Our distractions involve work, school, money, politics, laundry, podcasts, children, and celebrity breakups. Like a dog that is jolted from its thoughts by the appearance of a furry friend across the lawn, our biggest hindrance to sitting at the foot of the cross is the human equivalent of "*Squirrel!*"

"The constant distraction of our culture," writes Alan Noble, "shields us from the kind of deep, honest reflection needed" in order to see what God has done for us.[4] Or in the words of Andrew Sullivan: "If the churches came to understand that the greatest threat to faith today is not hedonism but distraction, perhaps they might begin to appeal anew to a frazzled digital generation."[5] Books on the atonement often miss this challenge. But it matters because Christ's saving work is not primarily a problem to be solved or a point of doctrine to be affirmed to stay in the Christian club. The cross is meant to lead us to worship, like the disciple Thomas when he encountered the scarred but risen Jesus, and then exclaimed: "My Lord and my God!" (John 20:28).

Arguing about atonement doctrine is one particularly dangerous distraction, especially amongst academics. To take one example, the idea of Jesus bearing the penalty for sin has been dubbed "divine child abuse" by some, while an opposing camp claims that emphasizing any picture of atonement other than "penal substitution" (I'll define that later) is as outrageous as renouncing the Apostles' Creed. This is especially odd since the early church never required Christians to choose one single understanding of how Jesus saves as most important. Unfortunately, the greatest act of reconciliation has turned into one more thing for Christians to fight over. When this happens, we sit beneath the cross, like disgruntled Roman soldiers, squabbling over Jesus's bloody garment but never looking up (John 19:23–24).

Conclusion

So before we explore the questions I have highlighted, I must conclude with one request: *Look up*. Look up at the cross that stands empty like the tomb. But look also to the throne of heaven where Jesus sits victorious over sin, death, and the devil. Look up from social media, from your smartphone, and from the

busyness of daily life to see Jesus in a new light. When
we do so, our faces will be illuminated. And in Paul's
words: "everything that is illuminated becomes a light"
(Eph. 5:13).

Each chapter of this book explores a particular
way Christ brings salvation. And each one returns to
some of the tough questions previously mentioned.
Unlike some modern treatments of the cross,
however, I do not raise questions in order to show that
the historic understandings of atonement are nonsen-
sical and barbaric. Not at all. If you're reading this
book in the hopes of getting my completely new and
original explanation of atonement, you'll be disap-
pointed. Because while we must take seriously the
questions and objections leveled, my conclusion will
be that Scripture and theology provide resources to
address those concerns without throwing the baby of
atonement out with the bathwater of bad analogies
and false assumptions.

There is mystery in atonement, but it is not a myth
that trades in superstitious nonsense. I believe that
Jesus saves. Hence, each chapter will explore a particular way in which Christ brings about salvation:

- By revealing the depth of our sin problems (chap. 1)
- By acting faithfully as the true Adam (chap. 2)
- By being judged in our place (chap. 3)
- By securing victory over death and the devil (chap. 4)
- By revealing God's love and pouring out his trans-
  forming Spirit (chap. 5)

Jesus does all that and more. That's why he's worth dropping everything to follow. These topics are complex, but my aim is to keep it simple. So each chapter comes in response to my daughter's question: "How does Jesus save us?"

Chapter One

Jesus and the Bigger Boat

Imagine if Quentin Tarantino directed a live-action version of *Finding Nemo* with only eleven dollars reserved for special effects. That's *Jaws*. If you're too young to remember the classic 1975 film, allow me to initiate you. The iconic scene begins with Roy Scheider's character (Martin Brody) chumming bloody bits of fish into the sea from the back of a dilapidated trawler. With a cigarette dangling from his lips, Brody turns from the ocean momentarily, just as a massive, tooth-filled head emerges from the water. The shark's colossal size inspires the famous line that becomes a prophecy of doom. Brody turns to the captain with a blank stare and proclaims: "You're gonna need a bigger boat."

Strange as it sounds, the cross of Jesus reveals the same reality. It shows us our collective human problem is bigger than we thought. So before we can speak of how Jesus saves, we must first ask why (and from what) we need saving.

Everybody Blames

Almost everyone admits there's something wrong with the world. Like the classic children's story *Everybody Poops*, another universal truth is "Everybody blames." Sometimes the tendency shows up in odd and extreme ways. When a massive hurricane slammed Florida and Texas, the actress Jennifer Lawrence prophesied that the devastation was Mother Nature's wrath on a nation that had elected a certain reality TV star as president. And a few years earlier, the president of a well-known Christian university attributed the 9/11 terrorist attacks to the sins of gays and lesbians.[1]

Why do people do this? There is something comforting about rendering our troubles meaningful as retribution. Retribution implies purpose. And it's invariably "the other side" to blame. Despite our talk of grace, we often find karma more appealing. One cable news network points the finger toward woke snow-flakes, millennials, social justice warriors, and illegal immigrants. But just check another news site and you'll hear that gun-lovers, science-deniers, and religious bigots are to blame.

Everybody judges. But which side is correct?

Into this partisan shouting match, the apostle Paul might walk—or rather, limp—and say, "You're both right." And also, "You're both *very* wrong."[2] Scripture shows that the problems we need saving from are more universal than one side of the political aisle. And they cannot be solved by simply electing the right people.

A predator lurks beneath the surface of our world and our skin. For this reason, the cross of Jesus isn't just a solution to our problems. It also functions like a warning indicator—a kind of "sin sonar"—to show how deep our issues are. The message, then, is simple: "You're gonna need a bigger boat."

Better Fall Saul

Paul came to this conclusion in an odd way. He fell. In the book of Acts, Paul (also called Saul) set out to persecute the followers of Jesus in a city called Damascus. In his mind, the biggest problem was bad Jews worshipping a crucified Messiah. But on his way to arrest these Christians, a bright light flashed around him. He fell to the ground and heard a voice call out: "Saul! Saul! Why do you persecute me?" In response, Paul asked: "Who are you, Lord?" Then he was shocked to hear this answer: "I am Jesus of Nazareth, whom you are persecuting" (Acts 22:6-8).

Here Paul gets an inkling of a shocking reality: The Lord of creation, the King of kings, the Messiah of Israel . . . is Jesus. And he died a criminal's death. *That's* how serious our problem was and is. It required nothing less than the sacrifice of God's beloved Son, nailed up to a Roman cross. For Paul, the catastrophic nature of the solution (the cross) revealed the catastrophic nature of our problem (sin, death, and the devil). But this is, admittedly, the opposite of how we normally reason.[3] We usually work from problem to solution.

Problem: I notice that my roof is leaking.
Solution: Call a home repair company and my insurance agent.

Problem: My clothes don't fit, and I get winded climbing stairs.
Solution: Start exercising or buy sweatpants and a ranch-style house.

Problem: My neighbor revs his muscle car at midnight while our baby is sleeping.
Solution: Ask him politely to stop. If he doesn't, learn karate.

The usual progression from *problem* to *solution* makes sense. But, occasionally, we are blindsided by a catastrophic solution. This unexpected and unsettling fix causes us to radically alter our perception of how bad the problem must have been. You go under the knife for a minor knee surgery, but when you awake the doctor tells you, "The bad news is we had to amputate; the good news is we got the cancer." A catastrophic solution is how Paul came to see the cross. God's fix was so terrible and unanticipated that it upended Paul's perception of how deep our problems were apart from grace.

Let's backtrack. Other Israelites in Paul's day had pointed the finger of blame at more specific culprits: (A) bad Jews, (B) bad spirits, or (C) bad Gentiles. But after his fall on the Damascus Road, Paul opted for a fourth option: (D) all of the above. The first choice was popular amongst the Pharisees (Paul's old sect). The next was taken by the Essenes (a vegan doomsday cult camped by the Dead Sea). The third was standard amongst the Zealots (revolutionary Rambo-Jews who saw Rome as the Great Satan). Each answer had merit. But each answer was too narrow. The diagnoses were like the selective blame games played by TV preachers, political pundits, and secular celebrities alike. Paul's jarring realization was that the sin-problem flows forth from each and every one of us, and its roots go far deeper than any other Jew had yet concluded.[4]

Paul traced the problem all the way to Genesis. In the first book of the Bible, one called "human" (*adam*) was led astray when tempted to distrust and disobey the Creator (Rom. 5:12a). In looking to Adam, Paul wasn't passing the buck to an ancient ancestor. He wasn't saying *everything* is Adam's fault alone. To clarify that point, Paul writes: "in this way death came to all people, because all sinned" (Rom. 5:12b). That's why "There is no difference between Jew and Gentile, for all have sinned and fall short of the glory of God" (Rom. 3:22b–23).

Sin is why even beautiful things—like sex and work and friendship—are now broken. This depressing reality is sometimes called "total depravity." Contrary to the way it sounds, total depravity does not mean that everyone is as bad as they could be. (You could be clubbing a baby seal right now with a bat you stole from underprivileged T-ball players.) A proper view of total depravity means that every *area* of life is bent by sin and human fallenness.[5] Paul says it this way in a passage that would make even the most disillusioned teenager seem chipper:

> What shall we conclude then? Do we [Jews] have any advantage? Not at all! For we have already made the charge that Jews and Gentiles alike are all under the power of sin. As it is written:

> "There is no one righteous, not even one;
>   there is no one who understands;
>   there is no one who seeks God.
> All have turned away,
>   they have together become worthless;
> there is no one who does good,
>   not even one." (Rom. 3:9–12; citing
>   Pss. 14:1–3; 53:1–3; Eccles. 7:20)

How's that for a downer? Nobody stencils those verses on a Christian T-shirt or inscribes them on a coffee mug.

The CAT Scan King

In medicine, a CAT scan (or CT scan) is used to diagnose problems that cannot be seen with the naked eye. It does so by combining electronic images to create a three-dimensional view of what's beneath the surface: bones, blood vessels, soft tissues. The rest of this chapter functions like a kind of CAT scan for the cosmos as a whole. It is an attempt to look at multiple layers of our problem, so we are prepared to see Christ's saving work in its full beauty.

Christians often fail here. In one segment of the church, the cross is simply Jesus taking our *penalty*. This approach implies that our problem is merely guilt demanding punishment. In another camp, the cross and resurrection are simply ways to victory and eternal life. In this diagnosis, the problem is our defeat by death and evil powers. In still another camp, Christ's work is seen as a powerful example of God's love that compels us follow. This is certainly accurate, but if left by itself it runs the risk of implying that a good example would be powerful enough to save us—as if standing over a coffin and showing an example of breathing could raise up the corpse.

In reality, we need several layers in this cosmic CAT scan.

If we only recognize one aspect of our problem, then our view of Jesus's work will be shallow. We will be like a patient who comes to recognize only *symptoms* of an ailment (the ache of loneliness, anger, or fear) without addressing the underlying diseases that cause them. So let's zoom in.

Death: The Final Enemy

In the Bible, "the last enemy to be destroyed is death" (1 Cor. 15:26). I began writing this chapter at a strange and frightening time in history: the early days of the COVID-19 pandemic. We learned new words: *lockdown*, *ventilators*, *social distancing*. And I remember the shock of learning that my next-door neighbor—a man named Tony—had died of the disease. He was in his forties, seemingly healthy, and he had two small children. The fear of death was everywhere. And even when the subject wasn't mentioned, it hovered silently in the background like the villain in a Harry Potter story: "He-Who-Must-Not-Be-Named."

My youngest son, Teddy, suffered his first asthma attack at the start of the pandemic. He was only two and I was scared. Should I take him to the ER and risk the strange new respiratory virus that might infect him? Or should I wait and gamble that his symptoms could get worse? After several sleepless hours, Teddy's breathing slowly improved. But in the days that followed, I noticed I was saying "I love you" more frequently—sprinkled liberally between commands to stop striking siblings and leaping from the furniture. "I love you, buddy." But what I meant was, *I'm scared you'll die.* Death is our great global pandemic. And the fear of it is not limited to COVID-19.

For this reason, the book of Hebrews says Jesus took on human flesh to "free those who all their lives were held in slavery by their fear of death" (Heb. 2:15). It is not just mortality that stalks us; it is the fear of death that haunts before the Enemy can pounce.

Some people try to repackage death to make it pretty. Several years ago, I sat on the platform for a college graduation at which a pastor quoted the late Steve Jobs: "Death is very likely the single best invention of Life," he said. "It is Life's change agent. It clears out the old to make way for the new."[6] That sounds nice. It makes death seem like a forward-thinking entrepreneur, fostering change and getting rid of old models. To speak of death in these sunny tones makes dead children, dead grandparents, and dead spouses sound like late-model Buicks that needed to be shuffled off the lot. Hogwash. Paul knew better. In Scripture, death is *always* an enemy—even though it results in an eternal "gain" for Christians (Phil. 1:21), and even when it comes at a ripe old age, or as a release from suffering.

But what is death? The answer might seem obvious. Even animals and children can tell when something has died. Recently, my children played with a pet frog so long that they literally killed it with their "love." They weren't fooled when I said the creature was just napping. But there are hints in the Bible that things are not so simple. Death comes in different forms. After Christ's resurrection, the New Testament writers begin to speak of it as "sleep" for Christians. "[W]e do not want you to be uninformed," writes Paul, "about those who sleep in death" (1 Thess. 4:13). This transformation does not make death pretty (the passage mentions grief explicitly). But it does mean that physical mortality becomes a temporary state for Christians, like the repose of Sleeping Beauty as we await our Bridegroom to awaken us.

Scripture tells of another death: a spiritual and relational one. The deepest and most problematic death isn't a stopped heartbeat or a decomposing body. The worst death involves our relationship with our Creator and our relationship with others. God told Adam that on that day you eat the forbidden fruit, "you will certainly die" (Gen. 2:17b). But of course, he didn't. Adam and Eve didn't keel over like the great mathematician and code-breaker Alan Turing, who supposedly committed suicide with a cyanide-laced apple. Adam and Eve lived physically for years after the fateful bites in Genesis 3. But that doesn't mean the serpent was right.

Death claims us while our hearts keep beating. Paul tells the Ephesians, "you were *dead* in your transgressions and sins, in which you used to live when you followed the ways of this world" (Eph. 2:1–2a, emphasis added). And to the church at Sardis, Jesus says, "I know your deeds; you have a reputation of being alive, but you are dead" (Rev. 3:1b). These texts reveal death as a problem that afflicts not just our bodies but our souls (Rev. 2:11). Death stems from a severed relationship with the one who is life: our Creator. This raises an important question: How alive are you right now?

The trouble with death is that it is not solvable by us. We may be able to delay death from a physical standpoint, but death turns out to be like winter in Russia: it's always coming. Eternal life is not a do-it-yourself project. You can't un-death yourself. And life's final enemy screams out from the abyss: "You're gonna need a bigger boat."

The Devil: Something Laughing in the Darkness

In the Bible, death is the domain of dark spiritual powers. Scripture says Christ died so that "he might break the power of him who holds the power of death—that is, the devil" (Heb. 2:14). But to speak like this risks ridicule. To modern people, talk of Satan and demons may sound spooky and superstitious. "Nothing commends Satan to the modern mind," writes Walter Wink. He is uncomfortable to speak of, like "a bone in the throat of modernity."[7] As proof, a recent survey claims that 40 percent of American Christians think the devil is *not* a "living being," but merely a "symbol of evil."[8]

Why is this? One reason may be that Christians have sometimes said foolish things about the devil. Satan is occasionally depicted as almost an equal power to God. And in a related fashion, Christians sometimes describe the devil in ways that make him seem all-knowing or all-present. The Bible doesn't do that. The fancy word for this error is "dualism" since it ends up with *two* spiritual powers (God and Satan) with nearly equal strength. Dualism makes good superhero movies, but it is bad theology.

As a kid growing up in the '80s and '90s, I remember listening to a song called "The Champion" by the Christian artist Carman. To understand the musical genre, imagine that an audiobook mated with an '80s synthesizer and the child grew up to do fight commentary for the Ultimate Fighting Championship. (If you're under thirty, YouTube it.) In "The Champion," the contest is literally described as a prizefight between apparently equal adversaries: Christ and Satan. The boxing match is overseen by God the Father, who utters such maxims as "You shut your face, I wrote the book!" Now, to be fair to Carman, the truth within the epic rap battle is that Jesus *is* victorious, but the misconception is that Satan is nearly as powerful as the divine Son of God.[9]

Between these two extremes—modern disbelief and a kooky dualism—resides the biblical position. Much mystery remains for Satan in the Bible. But some things can be said with confidence. Christians have always claimed that the devil is a creature. Only God is eternal. And since God is not the author of evil, the devil must have been created good originally. Unfortunately, as milk and mankind reveal when left alone for long enough—even good things can go bad. The Bible does not tell us exactly how that happened with the devil,[10] but, at some point, Satan and his minions fell.[11]

This does not mean, however, that we encounter demons flapping independently about the sky. In the Bible, dark spiritual power seems to need to be embodied in some way. Like the COVID-19 virus, evil spiritual powers are parasites that seek hosts. Thus, in Scripture, they are described as possessing persons, pigs, and political regimes. Satan enters Judas (Luke 22:3–6; John 13:27) who is called a "devil" (John 6:70). Satan gives his authority to the "beast" in Revelation, which is a symbol for the violent power of the Roman Empire (Rev. 13:4). And, on one occasion, some demons beg to be cast into a herd of swine (Matt. 8:31; Mark 5:12; Luke 8:32). It's weird and, perhaps, it seems unbelievable to you.

Yet this desire for possessive and devouring unions may be another sign that evil spirits were originally created good. After all, being fallen does not remove *our* desire to be one with other persons and groups. We still crave connection. But our brokenness renders these unions imperfect, codependent, and even abusive if we continue down dark paths. Fallenness turns union to possession and oppression. So, too, with evil spirits.

In J. K. Rowling's *Harry Potter*, Lord Voldemort seeks to unite his broken soul with physical objects (called horcruxes) in order to prolong his power. Analogously, evil spiritual power becomes incarnate in physical entities like exploitative corporate boards, violent or nationalistic political regimes, and profit-hungry tech companies that don't care what their anxiety-inducing algorithms do to people. This doesn't mean you can scream "Satan!" or "Possession!" every time you encounter discomfort or disagreement. (Some Christians have been too quick to smell sulfur around their enemies.) Nonetheless, you don't need to watch *The Exorcist* to see something demonic. Just look to the prescription drug companies that pumped 780 million painkillers into the state of West Virginia in just six years—an overdose-inducing feat that amounts to 390 pills per person.[12] Of course, those same opioids can be a blessing to suffering individuals. But the upside to this tragic problem merely illustrates my point: evil power is always a *corruption* of the good.[13]

But wait. Can we really expect modern people to believe in fallen spiritual powers? In one sense, that question is irrelevant. Evil spiritual powers do not depend on your belief for their existence. Satan does some of his best work in cultures that disbelieve in him. Still, it bears noting that our incredulity toward evil spirits has little basis in consistency. After all, belief in God still hovers near 90 percent in places like the United States. And as Alvin Plantinga notes, it's odd to affirm the possibility of *one* spiritual being (God) while drawing the line firmly against all others.[14] Imagine if we did this with mammals, dinosaurs, or aliens. I mean, if you are willing to grant there could be one . . . why not others?

Disbelief in evil spirits may sometimes betray a form of racial or nationalistic prejudice. *We are not like those superstitious people in the "third-world,"* says the sophisticated Western person. And in the same moment, we congratulate ourselves for having moved past other prejudices. African theologian Esther Acolatse calls out this inconsistency.[15] After all, what is so bizarre about believing that certain creatures could be created good before falling into rebellion? Look in the mirror for evidence of such a species.

Despite our questions about Satan, all of us have heard the voice of an accuser whispering destructive words within our ears. And very few of us can look at something like the Holocaust and not wonder whether whole nations may give themselves over to a kind of possession. Who among us can gaze upon our planet— so full of beauty and bloodshed—and not wonder if the cosmos itself has a backstory that is longer, darker, and more complex than we can fathom? In the face of this mystery, it is possible, as Robert Jenson notes, to hear the voice of something out there "laughing at us."[16]

We don't just have a death-predicament, we have a devil-problem too.

Sin: A Suicide Machine

But that doesn't mean we can say, "The devil made me do it." In Scripture, death is not merely the work of demons, it is also "the wages of sin" (Rom. 6:23). Unfortunately, for many modern people, sin also sounds like an old-fashioned concept, and especially when combined with the idea of divine wrath. Surely, you might say, we've moved past the old notion of a vengeful God who demands blood atonement? After all, when we attend a concert or sporting event, no one begins by leading an animal to the front and slaying it for all to see (Ozzy Osbourne notwithstanding). So why does Paul link death to "sins" that deserve "wrath" (Eph. 2:1, 3)?

One answer is simple. Sin kills. It dehumanizes people, destroys creation, and defames God's name. Sin always carries consequences—even if these repercussions are sometimes no more than the natural outcomes of our actions. Case in point: If you drink a keg of beer, you will suffer the wrath of a hangover. But that's hardly because God is sending vindictive wrath-rays toward your forehead. In other cases, God's wrath over sin does seem more active, personal, and forward-looking—as when Jesus threatened something *worse* than millstones around the necks of those who harm "little ones" (Luke 17:2). In either case, the result is clear: sin ultimately leads to death more surely than smoking to lung cancer, drunk driving to a DUI, Cheetos to orange fingers.

Still, the question remains: Why *must* death result from sin? If God is loving and powerful, why couldn't he simply overlook offenses? Why doesn't God simply forgive humanity just as a loving parent forgives their child without requiring death or blood atonement? I will return to the blood question in a later chapter. But suffice it to say that God doesn't get his jollies by watching creatures bleed out. The link between blood and atonement has a different purpose than cosmic sadism. Scripture teaches that God bears patiently with humans, even when we deserve judgment.

> The LORD is gracious and compassionate,
>   slow to anger and rich in love.
> The LORD is good to all;
>   he has compassion on all he has made.
>   (Ps. 145:8–9)

But love cannot ignore evil forever. Part of holy love is a zeal for justice. For example, we would all agree that to torture puppies, light a national park on fire, and abuse children *ought* to carry penalties. For a court to excuse these actions would not be compassionate. It would highlight a corrupt system and a complicit judge. Imagine looking at the horrific crimes of a man like Harvey Weinstein and saying something like, "Because I am merciful, I am going to let you off with a warning." No. Love and justice are not antithetical to penalties.

So, too, with sin. If there is a problem with our modern viewpoint, it is summed up by the medieval theologian Anselm, when he remarks to a questioner, "You have not yet considered the exceeding gravity of sin."[17] In the Bible, sin is not just a naughty action done by individuals or the breaking of an arbitrary rule. Sin piles up to become cosmic treason and it gathers steam to become an enslaving and oppressive power at both personal and systemic levels. When this happens, "Sin" takes on a capital S.

Parts of the Christian tradition (often conservative, white evangelicals) emphasize the *individual* aspects to our sin-problem: things like lying, lusting, and adultery. Meanwhile, other camps (often more progressive and diverse ones) emphasize the social and systemic sides of sin: things like institutionalized racism, abusive power structures, and governments that become "beast-like" in oppressive ways (Rev. 13).[18] In reality, sin is both personal and social.[19] It entraps us like an unbreakable addiction or a cruel slave master.

To focus *only* on systemic injustice allows individuals to justify their faults while decrying institutions. Conversely, to focus only on individual sin allows the church to justify complicity in systems, companies, and political parties that become oppressive, even while we congratulate ourselves for being faithful spouses or hardworking, God-fearing citizens.[20] Sin is both individual and systemic in its implications; hence, Scripture cares about both personal morality and corporate justice.

Shame: What It Feels Like to Be Naked

Another side effect of sin is not merely death, but also shame. After all, I have noted already that Adam and Eve do not drop physically dead when they disobey. Instead, they cover their genitals. That's shame for you. And if we miss this layer of our human problem, we will miss something crucial indeed. While guilt attaches to wrong actions, shame attaches to our personhood. Shame is the feeling not merely that I have done wrong but that I *am* wrong: worthless, unlovable, tainted, or defiled.[21] This makes shame insidious. Punishment or reparation may pay the debt of guilt, but shame clings to us like an ugly scar.

More terribly, we feel shame not just when we *do* wrong, but when others wrong us. The sexual assault victim feels ashamed of what was done to her. A bullied child feels shame for words shouted on the playground or posted on the Internet. One may be fat-shamed or slut-shamed regardless of one's weight or actions. And an elderly parent can feel shame for having lost his independence or the ability to control his bowels.

A biblical example of shame involves the woman Tamar in the Old Testament. We meet her in the reign of David. She was raped by her halfbrother, Amnon. And before being brutalized, Tamar cries out: "Don't force me! . . . Where could I get rid of my disgrace?" (2 Sam. 13:12–13). Tamar's question rings unanswered across college campuses, casting couches, and dark corners in the church basement. Where can one go to get rid of shame?[22]

Shame requires an unlikely cure. It can't simply be punished or defeated; it must be shared. It must be borne and then transformed, sometimes slowly, by an empowering and empathetic union—a union with one who reveals to us our true identity as precious beyond price. Disgrace requires a transformative entering in to the victim's experience. It cannot be fixed merely by punishing the guilty or forgiving the repentant.

It is no coincidence, then, that Jesus was crucified naked. Christian artwork can't handle this gritty reality, but the Gospels can: "They divided up his clothes by casting lots" (Matt. 27:35b). We know the Romans crucified their victims nude.[23] And the custom served a purpose: "The whole point of Roman crucifixion," writes Philip Cunningham, "was to reduce the victim to the status of a thing, stripping him of every vestige of human dignity, in order to discourage any challenging of the might of Rome."[24] Christ was therefore splayed out publicly before even his mother, female disciples, and a gawking crowd of friends and enemies alike. I can think of few things more humiliating.

Christ's naked death was even mocked in early graffiti. In what may be the earliest depiction of the crucifixion, a non-Christian artist derisively scratched a picture of a Christ-follower named "Alex" (Alexamenos) worshipping a figure on a cross. In the drawing, Jesus has the head of a donkey and the unmistakably naked buttocks of a human being. "Alexamenos worships his god," says the rude inscription. "Your savior is an 'Ass'" is the intended jest.

But shame was not the main takeaway of early Christians. Many early believers were slaves, women, and other marginalized persons in Roman society. In a stunning move, the church commandeered the shameful symbol of the cross. They hijacked the Roman propaganda and transformed it into a sign of triumph, empathy, love, and justice. Hebrews describes this holy hijacking when it asks its persecuted readers to fix their eyes on Jesus, who "endured the cross, scorning its shame" (Heb. 12:2).

Salvation is therefore spoken of as being *clothed* "with Christ" (Rom. 13:14)—a clothing that took place at baptism (Gal. 3:27). Hence the church began to baptize converts naked in imitation of the Christ who hung naked on the cross.[25] The meaning had nothing to do with the nudist exhibitionism of Woodstock or Burning Man. Rather, the metaphor of nakedness was transformed from a mark of shame to a metaphor of purity, innocence, and empowered vulnerability. To belong to Jesus was to be "naked" without shame (Gen. 2:25). "My Jesus bore my shame," one might hear across the centuries, from both Tamar and Alexamenos alike. But we are getting ahead of ourselves.

Conclusion

The point of this chapter has been only to highlight the problems that we face apart from Christ. What does Jesus save us from? To answer this question, I have undertaken a kind of 3D diagnosis of our human plight, like a cosmic CAT scan. Other layers could of course be added. But for the sake of time, these four "slices" (sin, death, Satan, shame) are sufficient to prove the iconic line from *Jaws*. When it comes to all the challenges that face us, "We're gonna need a bigger boat."

The early Christian writer, Augustine (AD 354–430), knew this. He had wrestled with unbelief, sexual misdeeds, a broken home, persistent pride, and bouts of despair. For all those reasons, he came to view the cross as a "wooden raft" that allows us to sail the sea of life and death. Since we could not sail to God ourselves, Augustine writes, "the one we were longing to go to came here." God made a "wooden raft for us to cross the sea on."[26] Astonishingly, however, Jesus did not just send the boat; he climbed aboard himself as our good Captain.[27] The cross of King Jesus, Augustine claims, *is* the bigger boat we've been needing. The atonement reveals how serious our problems are and it provides a way through churning waters.

ENGAGE THE TEXT

To reflect on the human predicament apart from Christ, read the following passages and ask God to speak to you through his Word:

- Psalm 14
- Romans 3:9–26
- 1 John 3:1–8

DISCUSS THE TEXT

1. This chapter argues that the cross isn't simply a solution; it also reveals how deep our problems actually are apart from God's grace. After all, if the Son of God had to take on flesh and die in order to redeem us, our plight must have been serious indeed.

   - Do you think most people still have a sense that they need a Savior?
   - Or have most people shifted their focus from transcendent problems (e.g., separation from God) to more temporal and immediate ones?

2. Which aspect of our human plight has most haunted you? Which one do you have a tendency to downplay or ignore?

   - Death
   - The devil
   - Sin
   - Shame

3. According to Scripture, death is "the last enemy to be destroyed" (1 Cor. 15:26).

   • How have you experienced the sting of death in your own life?
   • How did the early church shift its terminology on death, and what meaning did this shift convey?
   • Why is it good news that Jesus truly died, and not merely that he truly resurrected?

4. The devil is another aspect of our human problem.

   • The chapter describes the extremes of modern disbelief and kooky dualism on views of Satan. To which extreme are you most prone?
   • How has the devil been depicted or thought of in the culture, family, or tradition in which you were raised?
   • How is it that Jesus overcomes the devil? Can his method of overcoming Satan give you cues on how we can do the same?

5. This chapter describes sin as an offense against God, our fellow humans, and the created order God has made. Sin is also described as both individual and systemic.

   • Why do you think we are tempted to denounce some sins and not others?
   • In reflecting upon your background, are there some sins that you have tended to focus on, and others you have tended to ignore?

- Why does sin sometimes seem to take on a capital *S* within the Scriptures?

6. Shame is yet another side effect of sin. Hence, Christ comes to save us from it.

   - According to the chapter, what is shame and how is it distinguished from guilt?
   - How does Jesus deal with our shame problem?
   - Is there an area of your life where you feel burdened by the weight of shame? If you are comfortable, would you be willing to share that struggle in the context of a safe, Christ-honoring community?

Chapter Two

Jesus and the Severed Head

Julian of Norwich was dying. Her friends and relatives were sure of it. So as her end drew near, a crucifix was brought in for her to gaze upon. The year was 1373 and Julian was only thirty. But the fact that she had lived this long must have been considered fortunate. The Black Plague had ravaged her town when she was six, killing half its population. Now, however, it seemed that Julian would not be spared. Her breathing became ragged, her arms fell limp, and she cast a foggy gaze to the figure on the cross. Then it happened.

A crimson drop of blood rolled down from the crown of thorns. Then, suddenly, the Christ-figure came to life and started speaking just to her. Julian's account of these visions (composed after her surprising recovery) forms the first book ever written by a woman in English. They are also the most graphic descriptions of the cross in all medieval literature. There is no way to know, of course, whether Julian's visions should be

believed. Near-death experiences may produce hallu-
cinations. But it seems clear that Julian of Norwich
did believe them. She was even willing to risk being
burned alive as a heretic for daring to write about her
experience in the common tongue,[1] and despite the
scandalous fact that she was, you know, a woman.[2]

A key part of Julian's vision was a parable involving
a master and his servant. Julian believed the scene
revealed something important about how Jesus saves.
Unfortunately, the parable was also confusing. In her
vision, Julian saw a master call forth his servant and
send him on a mission. The servant ran joyfully to obey.
But then he fell into a ditch and cried out in agony.
Instead of rescuing his servant immediately, the master
looked on with contentment, knowing that his dear
servant would be rewarded far more than if he had
never fallen in the first place. Then, without explanation, the vision vanished.[3]

For twenty years, Julian pondered this ghostly
parable, not knowing what it meant. First, she thought
the servant might be Adam because he fell and
writhed in agony. But this did not match his perfect
obedience. Then she wondered if the servant might
be Christ. Yet this too raised questions: How exactly
did Jesus fall since he was sinless? Finally, after years
of prayer and contemplation, Julian believed that
God revealed to her the answer: The servant was *both*
Adam and Christ, because in the incarnation the Son
of God united himself to fallen humanity to experience our pain and blame, and to relive the human

drama faithfully on our behalf.[4] Somehow, Christ and Adam were connected.[5]

Jesus, the True Adam

This brings me to the first model of atonement in this book. It gives us at least a partial answer to one of the common questions people have about salvation: How is it possible for one person (Christ) to represent all others? We'll come back to that question, but for now, here is the big idea of this model of atonement: *Jesus saves as the new and true Adam, and the rightful "head" of all humanity.* This view of atonement is called recapitulation. But that rather clunky term speaks to how Jesus "re-headships" our fallen human family by reliving the human mission faithfully on our behalf.[6]

Biblical headship is not merely about being the boss. In the Scriptures, it can also be a way of referencing the *source* that is organically connected to the whole group.[7] Imagine a long and winding river. Like the headwaters of this river, what happens upstream invariably poisons or nourishes the entire downstream ecosystem. The river flows from its source as a unified thing. So although the water molecules may appear separate under a microscope, the headwaters flow into everything else. In Scripture, what happens to the "head" (whether Adam or Christ) affects the whole. Hence, Paul writes that "as in Adam all die, so in Christ all will be made alive" (1 Cor. 15:22).

Take a moment to consider how the Bible connects Christ and Adam. Both men are called "son of God" (Luke 3:22, 38), though Christ alone is truly divine. Both men act on behalf of *all* humanity. Both are tempted directly by the devil to distrust God's plan. And Christ's final temptation even takes place in a garden. The echoes of Adam and Eden continue with Christ's resurrection. This, too, takes place in a garden on the first day of a new week. The risen Jesus is called the "gardener" (John 20:15) and Christ leaves behind his grave clothes like an unshamed Adam robed in glory. In these ways and more, Scripture asks us to imagine Jesus as the true Adam, the source and head of a renewed humanity. In Paul's words: "Just as we have borne the image of the man of dust, we shall also bear the image of the man of heaven" (1 Cor. 15:49 ESV).

But Christ doesn't just relive the Adam story. The New Testament also teaches that God's family (Israel) is also bound in Adam's failure. Despite their calling to be part of God's rescue operation for creation, the Israelites also are enslaved to the sin and death that began with Adam's fall. Israel repeats Adam's folly—which is to say, Israel too is stuck "in Adam."

This point is important, because while Jesus sees himself as faithfully reliving the Adam story, he seems to see himself as reliving (again, recapitulating) the Israel story too.

Think of all the links between Christ's biography and the history of Israel. Like Moses, Jesus is born under the reign of a baby-killing king. Like Israel, Christ goes into Egypt and comes out with the catchphrase "Out of Egypt I called my son" (Hos. 11:1; Matt. 2:15). Like Israel, Christ is tested in the wilderness and led by the Spirit. Like Israel, he passes through the Jordan River to begin his kingdom-building work. Like Israel, his people are centered on a group of *twelve*, his agenda-setting sermon is given figuratively on a mount that is a nod to Sinai. And like Israel, Jesus undergoes the ultimate exile (death), only to return victorious with the nations streaming to him as King. In summary, Jesus saw himself as taking on the mission of *both* Adam and Israel, reliving (or recapitulating) those stories faithfully for others.

But this claim raises a problem. How can one ancient person (either Adam or Christ) stand in for us today and represent us? How does that work? As modern people, we often assume that we determine our own destinies. Because of individualism, I am tempted to reject the idea that I could be bound together with others as part of a common body or organism. I answer for my own mistakes. I am rewarded on my own merits. Or so I think.

We might call this the problem of our "bound-togetherness." The issue boils down to a simple question: How can a family head (whether Christ or Adam) reconfigure the destinies of so many other people? How can your life be mysteriously bound together with a person you have never met? How can the servant in Julian's trippy, deathbed vision be a symbol of *both* Christ and Adam? For many people, the contrast between modern individualism and this ancient view of bound-togetherness presents a problem for how Jesus saves. So let me tell you a more recent story.

The Lost Father

Abdulfattah Jandali ran a Mediterranean restaurant in California. He was a Syrian immigrant, balding and intelligent, with fierce eyes and round, wire-rimmed glasses. After coming to America, Jandali earned a PhD in economics. He got a job as a professor at the University of Michigan. He began dating a woman named Joanne, and she became pregnant. But despite his brilliance, Jandali was a flawed and restless man. So with Joanne still pregnant, he abandoned both his family and his career. The baby boy in Joanne's womb was given up for adoption.

Jandali later reunited with Joanne, they were married (briefly), and the couple had a daughter. But when the child was young, Jandali once again grew restless. He left and never returned. The baby girl grew up to be a famous novelist named Mona Simpson. And as an adult, she decided to seek out her long-lost father. *What was he like?* she wondered.

Why did he leave? Simpson hired a private investigator who tracked down Jandali, managing an eatery in California.

In a corner booth, Jandali told his daughter proudly of the places he had managed over the years—especially the Mediterranean one near San Jose. "That place was wonderful," he remarked. "All of the successful technology people used to come there. *Even Steve Jobs.* He was a sweet guy and a big tipper!" Mona Simpson's mouth fell open. What she never told her father was that Steve Jobs—the brilliant billionaire and founder of Apple Computers—*was* the baby Jandali had abandoned in the womb. And despite never knowing one another outside of those brief, oblivious encounters—the two men shared uncanny characteristics.[8]

Fathers shape us even in their absence. We inherit things. Like a sharp mind, a set of piercing eyes, and maybe even a taste for round-rimmed wire glasses. There is a mystery in what gets passed down. But in the case of Jobs and Jandali, the similarities do not stop there. Eerily, the founder of Apple Computers would also abandon his own firstborn child, Lisa, in the womb, at the exact same age Jandali had been when he left. What should we make of such surprising recapitulations? My claim is not that every aspect of our fate is predetermined by our past or our genetics. We can make choices—with God's help—to break certain cycles. But we are often more tied to others than we think as modern, Western individuals. In other words, as Jandali demonstrates: We are mysteriously bound up with our fallen forerunners.

An Apple with a Bite out of It

Steve Jobs's famed logo was an apple with a bite
missing. Yet there is another bitten fruit that figures
prominently in Scripture. In Genesis 3, humans reject
their calling to reflect God's character in the garden
they were called to "guard" (*shamar*; Gen. 2:15, author's
translation). This Hebrew word implies that though
Eden was very good, it was not yet perfect. Hence the
garden needed to be ordered and protected. That was
Adam's job.

Some scholars picture Eden like a beachhead of
shalom ("peace") carved out by God in a broader world
that had already experienced a cosmic disruption. Why
else would it need guarding? Why else would there be
a talking Tempter who we now know as "that ancient
serpent, who is the devil" (Rev. 20:2)? The first humans
occupy a territory that is good but dangerous. And
by falling for the serpent's temptation, the head of
humanity (Adam) is severed. Adam is cut off not just
from the tree of life but from the future God desired for
his people.[9] Just as with Jandali, fallen fathers cast long
shadows. Poisoned water flows downstream. The roots
affect the branches. No one sins in a vacuum.

It didn't have to be this way. Back in Genesis,
humans could have done what they were commanded
to do: guard the garden. After all, God gave them
authority to "rule over" animals (Gen. 1:26). And here
was one blaspheming the Creator (Gen. 3:4). Adam
could have done precisely what young David did when
he heard Goliath blaspheming Israel's God. He took

the fate of the people upon himself as their anointed head and soon-to-be king. What happened to David in that showdown with Goliath (in either failure or triumph) would carry over to the whole nation (1 Sam. 17:8–9). And in this case, as it was with Jesus, it was the Enemy's head that was severed.

Recapping Fallen Adam

This brings me back to Jesus. We have seen how Jesus is connected to Adam as the true head of all humanity. But how can this be? Christ was born long after Adam. And Jesus had no children. Wouldn't this make him more like the elbow of the human race? How can Jesus be the true head of all humanity? It's time to tackle more specifically the nature of our bound-togetherness.

Enter Irenaeus. Despite his strange-sounding name, Irenaeus was a Christian leader just after the time of the apostles (c. AD 180). Like Julian of Norwich, he was fascinated with the connection between Christ and Adam, and he saw this relationship as revealing something about how Jesus saves. Irenaeus noted that God made all humans in his image (Gen. 1:26). And despite sin, we retain that image even now. Since all persons have been stamped in God's likeness, our bodies have intrinsic value regardless of race, gender, wealth, or shifting beauty standards.

But the image of God is not just something we *have*—like blue eyes or an intolerance to dairy. The image of God is also something we *do*. Humans are called to "image" (or reflect) God to those around us.

It is a vocation and not just a possession. For these reasons, the image of God is one of the most important concepts in the Bible. Why is each human life precious beyond price? The image of God. Why is stewardship of the environment a sign of Christian maturity? The image of God. Why must racism, abortion, and sexual immorality be treated together as offenses against the way of Jesus? The image of God.

The image of God also explains *how* Jesus can represent all humans even though he is just one man. It's because even Adam was made in the image of God's Son—Jesus. The New Testament speaks of Christ as the true and perfect Image of God (2 Cor. 4:4; Col. 1:15). Though we are flawed reflections of God's character, Jesus is the perfect Image. As the second person of the Trinity, the Son of God preexisted Adam. Jesus is the eternal Son and the creative Word by which God made everything (John 1:1–3; 14). To use the analogy of a copy machine (which sounds pretty sacred, right?), we might say Jesus is the original Image that is used as the pattern to create all subsequent images. Every human who has ever lived was patterned and printed in the image of the true human—Jesus Christ.

This matters for atonement. For Irenaeus, since even Adam was made in the image of Christ, that makes Jesus the true head of all humanity. This means that at the *deepest root* of our expanding family tree—deeper than your grandparents, your weird uncle, or your ancient ancestors—there is not a fallen father. At the deepest root there is an obedient and perfect Son. Jesus is the image in which all people were created, and the head of his body, the church (Col. 1:15). Consider this rough diagram, which took thousands of research dollars to create, and an entire team of artists and geneticists.

The drawing shows that Christ is the founding head of the entire human race, like the unseen headwaters of a long and winding river. Because while Jesus was born near the middle of the human story, even Adam was patterned on the image of Christ.[10] For this reason, Paul states that just as Adam's disobedience led to the many being made sinners, so also through Christ's obedience "the many will be made righteous" (Rom. 5:19). Ultimately, Jesus isn't just one disconnected human

individual. Jesus is the rightful head of an interconnected human family.[11]

No matter what your past is like, this is good news.
In the words of Nichole Nordeman, God's love doesn't
"get hung up on the branches of family trees that bend
and sometimes break under the weight of our painful
histories. It's too busy at the roots. Where the soil is
soaked in mercy."[12] This is true because Jesus comes not
just as one perfect individual in the middle of history,
but as the new and true Adam who can empathize with
our pain and suffering, while lifting us out of the dirty
ditches where we've fallen.

Bound-Togetherness

The biblical view of how Jesus saves contradicts an individualism that views people like disconnected atoms.
In the words of Colin Gunton, individualism is "the
view of the human person which holds that there is so
much space between people that they can in no sense
participate in each other's being."[13] From the vantage
point of individualism, you and I are not connected. I
don't need you. And you certainly can't tell me what
to do. *That* would encroach upon my freedom. And in
individualistic cultures, freedom is the highest value.

Consider the way Americans sing our national
anthem. Pastor Tim Keller notes that at sporting events
or graduations, the cheering always begins during the
next-to-last line: "O'er the land of the free . . ."—at
which point, the singer elongates the final word to
several syllables with an extra high note on the end.

The song technically ends with a nod to "the brave," but both the vocals and the cheering highlight *individual freedom* as what Keller calls "the main theme and value of our society." So whenever there's a problem—say, an unwanted pregnancy or a global pandemic—the response is always the same: more freedom! My body, my choice.[14]

To be clear, a concern for individual human rights is a very good thing. But an imbalanced fixation on *individualism* has side effects. In particular, if my individual wants are perverted by sin and brokenness, then simply doing whatever I want—while screaming "Freedom!" like a *Braveheart* reenactment—will only lead deeper into addiction, self-destruction, loneliness, and despair. This isn't freedom. And an idolatrous elevation of *my* individual liberty can actually destroy the freedoms of others. The Bible describes this chaotic cycle in the book of Judges when it says that "Everyone did what was right in his own eyes" (17:6 ESV). To some modern readers, that verse might sound like utopia. Spoiler alert: It's not. It is a description of violence and enslavement, not liberation.

Some things that are essential for human flourishing challenge both our individualism and our definition of personal freedom. Allow me to explain. Let's start with three circles labeled *meaning*, *freedom*, and *community*.[15]

Humans need each of these three things. But to enlarge one circle to gargantuan proportions often requires the shrinking of at least one of the others.

Belief systems that give meaning also make demands upon your individual freedom. You cannot sleep with whomever you want. You cannot spend your money however you choose. You cannot ignore the poor, the immigrant, the orphan, or the unborn child. To have the meaning Jesus gives, your freedoms must be pruned into the shape of his kingdom.

So, too, for community. Ask any loving parent and they will say the deep communion of a family necessitates a shrinking of the individual freedom circle. Now that I have four small children, I cannot order my time however I choose. I cannot arrive home whenever I want, or watch *Die Hard* nightly after dinner. To be bound together with my wife and children means that my individualism must be molded into the image of Christ. When this happens, personal liberty doesn't go away (as totalitarian governments and Communist regimes have shown, that would be a very bad thing!). Rather, true freedom is to be defined by Christ: "You are not your own;" Paul wrote to the church at Corinth, "you were bought at a price. Therefore honor God with your bodies" (1 Cor. 6:19b–20).

The challenge of Christianity is to believe that "not being my own" is actually the most liberating news imaginable.[16] It means that we may be "in Christ" and bound together with others as his body. This perspective changes not only the way we view salvation, but the way we view everything.

Naturgemälde

Alexander von Humboldt was a busy guy. Born in the late 1700s, he was known as the greatest scientist-explorer of the age. There are more things named after Humboldt than for any other human who has ever lived.[17] (Which makes it weird that I had never heard of him.) As a young man, Humboldt crashed through dense foliage of islands off the coast of Africa; sailed to South America to peer into the yawning mouth of a volcano; enthralled Thomas Jefferson in Washington, DC (after chiding him for slavery); met Napoleon in Europe; and traversed Russia on his way to Siberia. He never stopped. And at each location, he collected specimens and took scientific measurements to understand our planet.

But it is Humboldt's spectacular three-foot-wide engraving, the *Naturgemälde*, that best encapsulates how he changed our vision of the world. *Naturgemälde* is a German term that means "painting of nature," but it also implies a sense of unity or wholeness by which we ought to view the world. The picture is of Chimborazo, a towering mountain in Ecuador that was thought to be the world's highest peak. Humboldt climbed the inactive volcano in 1802, on hands and knees with scientific instruments, across ridges that were only two inches wide. The engraving of the peak (later painted) shows a cross section of the mountain, both above and below the surface. Dozens of labels reveal the link between geology, plant life, and the climate—all embedded as parts of an interconnected whole.

Nature itself, Humboldt discovered, is a single organism, bound together in a complex web of relationships. Our minds tend to separate and categorize the various parts of our world as if they exist independently: fish, mountain, raindrop, Charlie Sheen. But that segregated view of the universe is a choice. And it is not what Humboldt came to see in all his travels. As his biographer would put it: "*Naturgemälde* unpeeled a previously invisible web of life. Connection was the basis of Humboldt's thinking."[18] Or in the memorable words of the American naturalist John Muir: "When we try to pick out anything by itself, we find it hitched to everything else in the universe."[19]

Bound-togetherness is also the basis of atonement. And the picture of redemption painted by Scripture is like a spiritual *Naturgemälde*. This first portrait of atonement (called recapitulation) says that Jesus can act on our behalf as our true head because, at our core, we are *not* disconnected individuals. Just as the *Naturgemälde* reveals a world that is interconnected, so too the image of God binds humanity together as an interconnected whole. Theologian Oliver Crisp refers to this as the union view of humanity: "The central claim of the union account is [that by] being united to Adam, I share in his sin; by being united to Christ I share in his righteousness."[20]

But how does one become *fully* united to Christ, the true Adam—beyond merely being made in his image?

Becoming the Bride

In Genesis we learn that Adam had a bride. Her name was Eve. And you may be wondering why Eve hasn't come up in this chapter. I've been saving Adam's bride for last. Not because she's unimportant. And not because she's more at fault than her husband. Adam's bride has something to teach us about atonement. Because while Eve was already connected to Adam by way of her creation (Scripture says she was made from Adam's rib, or side; Gen. 2:22), this *origin* is not the deepest union that they shared.

At their wedding ceremony Adam proclaimed his fuller *union* with her as "bone of my bones and flesh of my flesh" (Gen. 2:23). Years later, when Paul read this passage, he did not see just a picture of the first Adam or of human marriage. Paul saw a picture of what happens when *we* (the church) are united to the true Adam—Jesus the Christ. "This is a profound mystery," he wrote, "but I am talking about Christ and the church" (Eph. 5:32). We are united to the true Adam not just by our origin but by a marriage that comes by the Holy Spirit and faith. The Spirit of God enables us to say yes to Jesus, to give him our fidelity, and to be made one with Christ.

When we give allegiance to King Jesus, these are our wedding vows. And the Spirit applies the saving work that has already been accomplished. As the true Human, Jesus fully *accomplished* the "re-headshipping" of humanity. But for that work to be applied, the Spirit must unite us personally to our Bridegroom.

Otherwise, we would remain "in Adam." It's not enough to be connected to Christ by merely bearing his image. That would be like Adam's bride saying, "Thanks for the rib!" and then stumbling off to hang out with the serpent. Union is about more than creation. Union is about new creation. You must be wedded to Christ in the union that takes place by faith and by the Holy Spirit. We've got to become the bride for whom the true Adam laid down his life.

Conclusion

Like all of us, Julian of Norwich *was* dying. After all, death is a product of Adam's fall. Yet Julian's vision of a Christ who bound himself to fallen Adam (the severed head of humanity) reveals something important about how Jesus saves. He does so by reliving the human story faithfully on our behalf. When we are spiritually united with Christ as a bride to a bridegroom, what is true of him becomes true of us as well. We will now see how this union provides the foundation for all other views of the atonement to be covered in this book.

ENGAGE THE TEXT

To reflect on how Jesus saves by "re-headshipping" humanity as the new and true Adam, read the following passages:

- Genesis 3
- Matthew 4:1–11
- Romans 5:6–19
- 1 Corinthians 15:20–22

DISCUSS THE TEXT

1. This chapter deals with the question: How can one person (Jesus) represent all other humans in order to save us?

    - What questions or problems does this discussion raise in your mind?
    - What biblical ideas and passages were highlighted to address this question?
    - What arguments or examples from life today were used to help us break out of a radical individualism in which people are not seen as bound together?

2. This picture of atonement is often called "recapitulation." But that is a rather big and clunky term.

    - In simpler terms, what is meant by recapitulation, according to the chapter?

- What biblical examples were cited to support the idea of recapitulation (i.e., the head representing the whole)?

3. How does this chapter reveal the importance of Jesus's faithful life, and not merely his faithful death?

4. To explore our bound-togetherness, the author highlighted three circles labeled *meaning*, *freedom*, and *community*.

   - What basic claim was made regarding the relationship between these central human needs? Do you agree? Why or why not?
   - In examining your own life, is there one of these circles that gets supersized in ways that become problematic? How so? What might God be calling you to change about this area of your life?
   - How does Jesus redefine the "freedom" circle by way of our bound-togetherness with him? Why is this actually good news?

5. Why is it crucial to note that Jesus's union with his people (the church, his bride) must be *applied* personally, even though it has been accomplished universally?

6. Part of this chapter dealt with fallen fathers; both Adam and others, like Abdulfattah Jandali. How might it change your view of yourself and your past if you truly believed this sentence from the chapter:

"At the deepest root of our expanding family tree—deeper than your grandparents, your weird uncle, or your ancient ancestors—there is not a fallen father. At the deepest root there is an obedient and perfect Son."

Chapter Three

Jesus and the Judged Judge

Epstein didn't kill himself." Those words ran like wildfire through the Internet in 2019. In August of that year, Jeffrey Epstein, the multimillionaire and registered sex offender, was found dangling and dead inside his federal prison cell. Outrage followed. Security cameras were not functioning. Guards were elsewhere. And many wondered why a suicide watch on Epstein had recently been suspended. But the indignation over Epstein's death was not limited to those who thought he had been murdered.

Another frustration was that Epstein could not now be held *officially* accountable for his evil acts in abusing young girls in an international sex-trafficking operation. He was dead, but the world felt justice had not ultimately been served. In our eyes, some crimes are so heinous that they cry out for a severe and public penalty—an official sentence handed down and carried out. I note this reality not because I have any personal theory regarding Jeffrey Epstein, but because it connects to a much older debate over the hanging of another famous convict—Jesus of Nazareth.

The Judge Judged in Our Place

In answer to my question: "How does Jesus save us?" one of the most common responses is to say the following: *Jesus saves by bearing the penalty for human sin in our place.* Thus, this model of atonement deals with the demands of justice. When Paul summarizes the gospel, he mentions first that "Christ died for our sins according to the Scriptures" (1 Cor. 15:3). And when he explains why there is no condemnation for Christians, it is because God "condemned sin in the flesh" of the Messiah (Rom. 8:3). God did so to demonstrate his *justice*, because "he had left the sins committed beforehand unpunished" (Rom. 3:25).[1] The Bible links Christ's death to the penalty for human sin, despite the fact that Christ was not a sinner.

But how could that be? How could it be good news that an innocent person (Jesus) died for the sins of the guilty? To feel the force of this question, imagine a very different ending to the Epstein saga. Suppose a judge had heard all the evidence against Epstein—the trafficking, the blackmail, the child abuse—and then handed down a sentence: death. Then imagine if this same judge had stepped down from the bench, walked into the prison where Epstein languished, and allowed *herself* to be hung in his place. Would we call that justice? Would Epstein be allowed to go free? And would this strange penalty exchange be good news to all who heard it, including Epstein's many victims? The answer to all these questions would seem to be no! How could it possibly be good news that the judge was hung in place of the wrongdoer?

Yet Christians claim precisely that.[2]

At the level of parking fines or overdraft charges, the idea of a penalty exchange may sound reasonable. After all, a generous friend may volunteer to pay my debt after I foolishly left my Honda Civic unattended by an expired parking meter. All that matters is that the fine gets paid. But when we move to capital punishment, it's unclear that this exchange makes sense. The problem is simple: we tend to think of sin and punishment as rightly sticking to the perpetrator. Death penalties are not like tradeable coupons or unused frequent flier miles. You can't shift them however you like. And in the case that such a swap is attempted, it would be the opposite of justice. Right?

Prince Brat

Like all fifth graders in the 1990s, I was forced to read *The Whipping Boy* by Sid Fleischman. In this fictional kingdom, no one was permitted to punish the future monarch, the aptly named Prince Brat, with a swat on his royal backside, so the impoverished orphan Jemmy was selected to receive the prince's spankings. By seeing Jemmy punished in his place, the hope was that the prince would feel bad, repent, and become a good boy. (Spoiler: It doesn't work.)

The premise of *The Whipping Boy* is meant to jar us. Our children are meant to ask how there could be such an unjust kingdom. Who would think that the practice of violent penalty-swapping would be a good and just way to bring about remorse and repentance? This same logic is sometimes used to show that atonement by way of penalty exchange (often called penal substitution) is abusive, unbiblical, and just plain weird.[3] To be honest, the critiques are sometimes right, at least when applied to mangled versions of this model.

Not all versions of this atonement explanation are worth saving. Some *are* downright appalling, unscriptural, or even pagan! God the Father has even been described in ways that make him seem like an abusive dad who must vent his rage and hatred upon an innocent son, so he can forgive us.[4] The vast swath of the Christian tradition—from John's Gospel, to John Calvin, to John Wesley—never claimed this nonsense. Scripture never says that God tortured Jesus, that the Father hated Christ upon the cross, or that the Father and the Son could *ever* be pitted against each other.[5] To say otherwise is to deny the doctrine of the Trinity.[6]

But to dismiss abusive versions of this model does not mean we can drop the biblical idea that Christ willingly bore the divine judgment for human sin. We need to move past the crass caricatures if we are going to grasp this aspect of how Jesus saves.

The Sacrificial CEO

Even today, there are cases in which we recognize the justice of one person bearing a penalty for others. Take the example of a CEO who chooses to step down for infractions done by lower members of her company. Crimes were committed, investors were defrauded, a copy machine on the seventh floor was used for, well, nefarious purposes. And although this CEO did not perpetrate the misdeeds, the fact that she is the head of the company may make it right that she willingly accepts a consequence for wrongs done by her corporation.

Corporation. That word contains a clue about how Christ's penalty-bearing avoids the justice problem. Corporation comes from the Latin word for body: *corpus.* And as I argued in the last chapter, Jesus steps into history not as a disconnected individual, but as the rightful head of a bound-together family—God's image-bearers: those made in the image of Christ. Our bound-togetherness matters for atonement, and specifically for the idea that Jesus can justly bear the judgment for our sin.

Scripture is clear that random penalty-swapping is *not* okay.[7] Proverbs states that "Acquitting the guilty and condemning the innocent—the LORD detests them both" (17:15). So when we say that Jesus graciously bore our penalty, we are not espousing a whipping-boy theology. The cross may be a scandal to modern sensibilities, but it is not that blundering or simplistic. What exactly happens in Jesus's death must be understood through the lens of Israel's covenant and sacrifice. Now to unpack those ancient concepts.

A Smoking Firepot

One of my jobs as a pastor is to officiate at weddings. I'm preparing for one soon, in fact, between two of my former students. They are so in love that it would make you sick. They're actually *excited* to spend their lives together—for richer or poorer, in sickness and in health. I can relate. Because after all these years, I still feel that way about my wife. But when they finally stand up in front of their friends and family, I will have to splash some cold water on the occasion. "Marriage," I will say, "is not simply a contract; marriage is a covenant." And in the ancient world, it wasn't metaphorical cold water that got thrown into the ceremony, it was warm blood. Covenants included sacrifice.

Consider Genesis 15. This is one of the most important covenant passages for understanding Christ's saving death. Roughly two thousand years before the birth of Jesus, YHWH appears to a man named Abraham (then called Abram). God promises to be Abraham's Shield and great Reward (v. 1). And God tells him that his offspring will outnumber the stars (v. 5), despite the fact that he and his wife are old and barren. No matter. "Abram believed the LORD, and he credited it to him as righteousness" (v. 6).

God takes Abraham's faith—or what we might call his believing-allegiance—and grants him the status of a faithful partner in the covenant.[8] Then things get weird. To seal the arrangement, God asks Abraham to bring a heifer, a goat, a ram, a dove, and a young pigeon. Not an old pigeon, mind you. Not a geriatric yard bird that had been around the block and left his mark on park benches through the years—a young pigeon—which raises questions about how one ascertains the agedness of said pigeon. But I digress.

Abraham did it. He killed the animals, he cut the larger ones in half, and he arranged the pieces like a serial killer trying to send a message. But that's not actually what's going on. The carcass symbolism was standard practice in the ancient world. Covenants were sealed with blood, and meaning seeped through the gory ceremony. As a part of this symbolism (or from chasing youthful pigeons), Abraham fell asleep. Genesis says that "a thick and dreadful darkness came over him" (v. 12). Then God showed up.

> When the sun had set and darkness had fallen,
> a smoking firepot with a blazing torch appeared
> and passed between the pieces. On that day
> the LORD made a covenant with Abram . . .
> (Gen. 15:17–18)

Like marriage today, ancient covenants brought two parties (like a king and a commoner) into a bonded relationship of union and obligation. Covenants included stipulations; they included promises; and they included penalties for breaking them. That's where the dead animals come in. Typically, the lower ranking covenant partner (or perhaps both parties) would walk between the cloven carcasses as a way of saying, "May this happen to me and more if I break the words of the covenant."[9] Imagine if we did that in weddings now:

> "Now Bill, you repeat after me . . ."

> *If I should cheat on my wife,*
> *or even mention that she hath "gained a few*
> *pounds,"*

may my flesh be torn by rabid pit bulls, while
women mock my male-pattern baldness!

In ancient covenants, this was no laughing matter. To pass between the pieces was to put one's life and honor on the line. But Abraham doesn't do that. Remember, he's passed out on the ground like a tired grandpa after Thanksgiving dinner.

To quote Markus Barth: "God alone . . . walks the bloody road between the carcasses."[10] We know it's God by the way he is described. Or rather, we know it's God by the way he is *not* described. The Old Testament avoids visual descriptions of God's form. Such visual depictions were called "idols." So instead of describing what God looked like, Genesis describes the smoking firepot and blazing torch that God was carrying.[11] The depiction avoids idolatry, but it also points forward to a future atonement through divine penalty-bearing.

God places *himself* on the line by passing through the pieces. God signals his willingness—indeed, his intention—to bear the covenantal curse that should fall on Abraham and his offspring if they should be unfaithful to their vows. This curse involved not just death (Rom. 6:23), but exile from the land God promised (Deut. 28:64). That's what death is in Scripture: exile from the land of the living. Way back in Genesis, God shows that he will bear the penalty for the sins of his people. Like a spouse who accepts the partner's past and future debts because the two have become one, God will bear the covenantal curse for his wayward bride.

From *Aqedah* to YHWH's Servant

Now let's look to three other Old Testament passages that point forward to Christ's judgment bearing death. A few chapters after God passes through the pieces, we find the *Aqedah* (Gen. 22). This Hebrew word describes the binding of Abraham's beloved son, Isaac, on a sacrificial altar. Although the story rightly sounds horrific today, the key lesson is that God himself will provide a sacrifice for his people: "God himself will provide the lamb for the burnt offering" (v. 8). And sure enough, God does. Abraham is commanded to sacrifice a ram "instead of his son" (v. 13). Here is a clear reference to sacrifice as substitution (an offering of one thing instead of another). The New Testament takes up this imagery to point to Jesus, the beloved Son who, like Isaac, carries the wood of his own offering up a different hillside (John 19:17).

Next comes *Yom Kippur*. This Day of Atonement was the one date in the Hebrew calendar in which sacrifice was made for the willful sins of Israel. A key portion of the ceremony involves two goats. The first goat was sacrificed before the Lord upon the altar while the other animal (the "scapegoat") had Israel's wickedness confessed over it before being exiled outside the camp to bear away the sins of the people (Lev. 16:21–22). Much remains mysterious about the Day of Atonement.

Yet it is likely that both goats point toward Jesus and his judgment-bearing death that is simultaneously a form of exile. Like the first animal, Christ dies in the place of the people. And like the second, he is led outside the camp, to bear away our sins. There is both penalty-bearing and substitution in the Day of Atonement, both sacrificial death and a forgiveness after exile.[12]

Finally, we arrive at Isaiah 53. Here we read of a Servant of Yahweh who is "pierced for our transgressions" and "crushed for our iniquities; the punishment that brought us peace was on him, and by his wounds we are healed" (v. 5). The most astonishing feature of this passage is the merging of sacrificial themes ("the LORD makes his life an offering for sin" [v. 10]) with references to what is apparently a human victim who takes on the penalty for the people's sin. The New Testament picks up these cues and applies them directly to Jesus.[13]

The Ransom and the Cup

Christ was looking back at Isaiah's Servant when he proclaimed that "the Son of Man did not come to be served, but to serve, and to give his life as a ransom for many" (Mark 10:45). Jesus seemed to see himself as living out the vocation of the Servant to offer his life for the sins of the people.[14] In speaking of his suffering and death, Jesus saw the ordeal as more than just a tragedy, a triumph, or even a loving example. He used biblical imagery to suggest that he was enduring the judgment

for the sins of Israel. We see this in his anguish over the
cup he would choose to drink.

Hours before his death, Christ cried out, "My
Father, if it is possible, may this cup be taken from
me" (Matt. 26:39a). The cup was an image of God's
judgment upon human sin (Ps. 75:8; Rev. 16). Far from
an explosive or sadistic rage, however, the metaphor
speaks to God's patience, love, and justice. The idea
is that human evil eventually accumulates a penalty,
like wine continually poured into a glass that must
ultimately overflow. Thankfully, the Christian God is
not like Zeus. He does not randomly zap people for
no reason. Nor does God's anger have a hair trigger
to smite when we mess up. God is slow to anger and
abounding in love (Ex. 34:6). Still, it is *love* that necessitates that evil be dealt with rather than ignored. It
would be unloving for a judge to look at a serial abuser
like Jeffrey Epstein and say, "Because I am merciful, I
have chosen not to punish you."

Justice and compassion go together. God's wrath is
therefore nothing other than the faithful outflow of his
holy love. The cup of judgment represents God's settled
opposition to the sin and evil that destroy his beloved
creation.[15] The covenant had always proclaimed that
evil must be judged (Gen. 15; Deut. 28). And it is this
cup of judgment that Jesus chose to drink on behalf of
us. He saves by graciously and willingly taking on the
penalty that our sin deserved.

That's why Paul says there is "no condemnation for those who are in Christ Jesus" (Rom. 8:1).
Condemnation is God's ultimate judgment upon sin.

Yet there is none of that for Christians because God condemned our sin "in the flesh" of our Messiah (v. 3). The Lord did that "in order that the righteous requirement of the law might be fully met in us" (v. 4). The language in this passage is important for avoiding the abusive versions of penalty-bearing mentioned earlier. Note that it is *not* the Son who is the object of God's condemnation or hatred. Instead, it is *sin* that is condemned in the flesh of Jesus. Sin, not the Son, is the focus of divine judgment on the cross.

The Cross and Chemotherapy

To grasp this distinction, consider an analogy. Suppose a doctor tells you that you have an aggressive form of cancer. You did nothing to deserve this horrible disease. But the cancer is there now in your flesh by virtue of your family history, your genetics, and your environment. The only cure is a form of chemotherapy: a poison you must drink. The treatment's goal is not to torture you or make you suffer (though you will suffer by taking it); the intent is only to deal with the cancer bound up in your body. So, too, when Scripture says that God condemned sin in the flesh of the beloved Son (Rom. 8:3).

That's the difference between an abusive whipping-boy theology and the biblical notion that Christ willingly bore the covenantal consequences of our sin because he is bound up *with* his people as the head of a unified body. At this point we come to the interplay

between representation, substitution, and incorporation in atonement.

Representation—In our place, **for** us.

Substitution—In our place, **instead of** us.

Incorporation—In our place, **with** us.

Because Christ is the head of all humanity, he can
truly represent us all. He acts "for us" (representation)
because we are bound up "with" him (incorporation).
But because we are different persons, we do not *experience* the torment of the cross, nor can we take credit for
it (substitution). All three of these dynamics are true in
different ways, and these three aspects of Christ's work
show how the current chapter sits atop the prior one
on recapitulation.

Recapping Recapitulation

In the last chapter I claimed that Jesus can act on
behalf of all humanity because he is the true Adam, the
true Israel, and the image-bearing head of all humanity.
This interconnected view of reality is assumed in
Scripture, but it seems strange today because it challenges our modern individualism. What we need is a
more connected ("hitched together") view of the world,
which I illustrated by way of Steve Jobs's biological
father, Alexander von Humboldt's *Naturgemälde*, and
my amazing drawings. Remember?

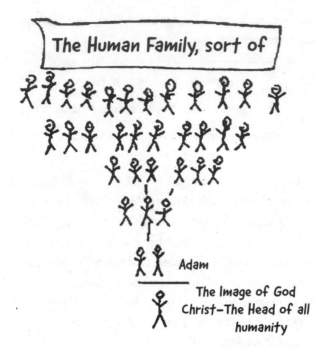

The Human Family, sort of

Adam

The Image of God
Christ—The Head of all
humanity

Now it's time to take these insights and apply them to what I've called the "justice problem" of Christ's death. How can an innocent person (Jesus) justly accept the consequences for the guilty? How can Christ's judgment-bearing death not devolve into the bizarre scenario I described earlier with regard to a judge hung in place of Jeffrey Epstein?

The answer is that Jesus is unique. He's not like other human individuals. Christ *can* act on behalf of others because all people are mysteriously bound up *with* him as the true Adam. For this reason, Scripture claims that "He is the atoning sacrifice . . . not only for [our sins] but also for the sins of the whole world" (1 John 2:2). Jesus is not just a random guy amongst other random individuals.

Rather, the entire universe is bound up with the Son of God, for "in him all things hold together" (Col. 1:17).

That's why Paul can say he has been "crucified with Christ" (Gal. 2:20). From his ancient, Jewish perspective, what is true of the head is true of the body. The head can act for the whole. That's why Jesus can die for the sins of the whole world. And that's the answer to the justice problem. Bound-together union is the foundation of Christ's penalty-bearing death.

The Dotted Line

But wait a minute. If Jesus dies for the sins of the whole world, does that mean all people are already saved? Not quite. There are salvation passages in Scripture that sound quite universal. Acts says that God will one day "restore everything, as he promised long ago through his holy prophets" (3:21). Romans tells that "one righteous act resulted in justification and life for all people" (5:18). Second Corinthians celebrates that "God was reconciling the world to himself in Christ" (5:19). And Colossians states that God was pleased "to reconcile to himself all things . . . by making peace through [Christ's] blood" (1:20). These texts proclaim that God has clearly done something for *all humanity*, and even all creation, in the Christ event.

But there are other biblical statements (often from the mouth of Christ himself) that make it clear that not every person will ultimately accept God's universal achievement.[16] That's why almost the entirety of church tradition has rejected "universalism"—that is, the belief that every human will ultimately be saved.[17] To explain how this paradox connects with Christ dying for the sins of the whole world, it's time for one last amazing illustration. Gird your loins.

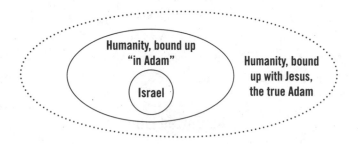

The dotted line around *all humanity* "bound up with Jesus" is important in its symbolism. It is real but not absolute. It is like a fence that can be overstepped, a border than can be crossed, or a Father's house that can be fled at the cost of tears and patient waiting for the prodigal's return. Jesus really does die for the sins of the whole world (1 John 2:2). God really does desire that all people would be saved (1 Tim. 2:4; 2 Peter 3:9). And Christ really does accomplish something universal in his death (Col. 1:20).

But that universal accomplishment must be *applied* and sustained for individuals by the Holy Spirit. That happens when you give your allegiance to Christ as King. The prison doors have been flung open, but some may choose to sit inside the dreary cell rather than step out in freedom. Scripture teaches that it may even be possible to poke a head, a foot, or *more* across that line, only to pigheadedly sulk back inside. This is called "apostasy" in church tradition, and it refers to the possibility of saying yes to Jesus at one point, only to reject him in a flagrant way. That's why Scripture gives numerous warnings to members of the faith community about the need to "remain" in Christ, lest we "fall from grace" and find ourselves "cut off" from him after having made a "shipwreck" of our faith.[18]

These passages are not aiming to cause anxiety for Christ-followers. After all, the same Paul who warns of falling away also expresses confidence that the God who began a good work in you will carry it to full completion (Phil. 1:6). The dotted line, then, is not some hidden mark that you unknowingly stumble past every time you sin. It is more like a high wall that one must deliberately scale, even while a strong and loving Christ throws himself across the path to hell and says, "Over my dead body!"

The Other Epstein

Here at the end of the chapter, there is one aspect of the justice problem that I have yet to cover. It involves what Christ's judgment-bearing death has to say to the victims of terrible injustice. So let's conclude with that.

Whatever happened to Jeffrey Epstein, Larry Nassar *didn't* kill himself. (Or at least he hadn't at the time I wrote this chapter.) The former doctor is a serial rapist and abuser who molested dozens of little girls and young women at Michigan State University and U.S.A. gymnastics. Powerful people covered for Nassar, just as others did for Epstein. They shamed and smeared his victims, intimidated them into silence, and called them liars and troublemakers when they were only crying out for help and justice.

A few years ago I sat and listened to a presentation on atonement by one of Nassar's victims: Rachael Denhollander.[19] Rachael is now a lawyer, and alongside her husband, Jacob, her claim was that far from being abusive, a proper understanding of Christ's penalty-bearing death actually upholds justice, and offers hope to victims. The cross does not display one member of the Trinity hatefully punishing another. Far from it! The cross reveals the one God—Father, Son, and Spirit—moving in harmony to save humanity and demonstrate how seriously God takes sin.[20] God hates evil. And this hatred of injustice is good news for victims who have seen abuse swept under the rug.

Rachael argued that Christ's death reveals that justice and forgiveness actually belong together. Yes, God forgives. And, yes, we must too. But that does not mean that justice should be brushed aside, or that certain penalties can be simply waived because we believe in mercy and forgiveness.[21] Forgiveness should not be weaponized as a get-out-of-jail-free card for oppressors. Rather, to quote the Denhollanders:

> In every possible scenario in Christian theology, the reality of evil and need for justice is upheld. Either divine punishment will be meted out on the individual who has done the wrong, or it is taken up by God himself, but even perfect, divine forgiveness rightly seeks and upholds the need for justice.[22]

Finally, Rachael shared how Christ's sin-bearing death redefines justice by upending sinful power dynamics. Rather than the strong exerting their might and wealth over the weak, as happened with Epstein and Nassar, Scripture reveals an Almighty One who *becomes weak and poor* for others (Phil. 2:6–8), even bearing the curse of the covenant for us. The all-powerful God identifies with victims, enters our brokenness, and repudiates the myth that power must be wielded exploitatively. Christ's suffering Servanthood (Isa. 53) is not the antithesis of biblical justice, it is its definition. Furthermore, it reveals the way *we* should steward our power and privilege.[23] It's no wonder then that perhaps the most powerful biblical text on justice comes in another passage about Isaiah's suffering Servant (Isa. 42:1–9).

In her victim impact statement, Rachael framed her testimony around a single question: "How much is a little girl worth?"[24] She asked hearers, and especially the judge, to look around the courtroom and ask that question before sentencing Larry Nassar. But she offered more than righteous anger toward the man who hurt her. Looking straight into Nassar's eyes she said:

Should you ever reach the point of truly facing what you have done, the guilt will be crushing. And that is what makes the gospel of Christ so sweet. Because it extends grace and hope and mercy where none should be found. And it will be there for you.

I pray you experience the soul-crushing weight of guilt so you may someday experience true repentance and true forgiveness from God, which you need far more than forgiveness from me—though I extend that to you as well.[25]

In the end, Rachael and the other victims requested and received the maximum possible sentence for Nassar's crimes. Because as Rachael noted, the answer to the question "What is a little girl worth?" is "Everything."

Conclusion

The judgment-bearing death of Christ is also the answer to that question: "How much is a little girl worth?" Everything. Christ's sin-bearing death reveals how serious are the demands of the covenant in the face of human wickedness across countless centuries—over battlefields, Klan rallies, gossip sessions, playground bullying, spousal abuse, and environmental destruction. The cross reveals how seriously the triune God takes the demands of justice and the desire to be merciful, even to the likes of Epstein, Nassar, and *you* yourself. The Lord himself has promised that justice will be done one way or another, and the Lord himself has passed through the pieces.

ENGAGE THE TEXT

To reflect on the biblical idea that Jesus saves by willingly bearing the judgment for sin in our place, read the following passages and ask God to speak to you through his Word:

- Isaiah 42:1–9, 53
- Mark 10:45
- Romans 3:25–26; 8:1–4
- 1 Corinthians 15:3–4

DISCUSS THE TEXT

1. Have you ever struggled with how Jesus (an innocent person) could justly die for the sins of the guilty? How have you sorted through this question?

2. What biblical ideas did the chapter set forth to help with that so called justice problem? To jog your memory, consider the following proposals:

   - Jesus as the true Adam, the head of all humanity
   - Genesis 15 and God's decision to pass between the pieces
   - The "bound-togetherness" of the universe in Christ, the Son (Col. 1:17–18)

3. How does this model of atonement hold together justice and mercy? And why is that move an important one in order for God to be truly loving?

4. Why did the author claim that sin, not the Son, is the focus of God's judgment on the cross? (See Rom. 8:3 for biblical support.)

   • How does this distinction help us avoid undermining the doctrine of the Trinity?
   • How does it help us avoid undermining God's holy love?

5. Why did Rachael Denhollander claim that Christ's judgment-bearing death is good news for victims who have seen their abuse swept under the rug?

6. How might your view of God or of your past be different if you truly believed that "there is now no condemnation for those who are in Christ Jesus" (Rom. 8:1)?

Chapter Four

Jesus and the Double Deathblow

How does one win by losing? Several years ago, I was asked to serve as cornerman for a cage fight. It happened this way: At the time, my close friend and workout partner decided to take his first bout in mixed martial arts (MMA). I was not *supposed* to be the cornerman, mind you, because I have never been in a fight that didn't involve the words *nerf* or *pillow* in front of it. But as I was eating dinner beforehand with another friend, the phone rang: the official cornerman had been called in to work, and we were in.

In the bowels of the venue, I attempted an inspiring prefight pep talk like in *Rocky* or *The Karate Kid*. Unfortunately, it came out more like, "Maybe, try to hit him in the face." Then we walked to the cage with the music blaring and lights illuminating the thick necks of people in the crowd. At the opening bell, my buddy rushed forward to execute my proposed strategy of "maybe punching him in the face"—at which point the other fighter shuffled backward, reset suddenly, and landed a crushing head kick to my friend's lower jaw. He fell like a sycamore, knocked out cold.

Concussions are strange things—and frightening. Apparently, you don't remember them. It's as if someone does a hard reset on your nervous system and your brain doesn't store the memory. Thankfully, my friend was soon okay—or, as okay as anyone who takes up cage fighting in their thirties—but our careers in MMA and "corner-manning" were done. After the referee raised the other fighter's hand in victory, we shuffled to the locker room where he proceeded to ask the same question every five minutes for the next hour: "So . . . what happened?" Since he didn't remember, I smiled and told him that he'd won.

Victory by Death?

But of course, he didn't. It would be foolish to speak of such a brutal loss as a victory. Getting knocked out is not what winning looks like in cage fights. And combat athletes don't have patience for our modern metaphors of moral victories and participation trophies. *Hey Drago, you're a winner on the inside!* No. Victory doesn't work that way in MMA; nor did victory work that way in the rough-and-tumble world of the Bible. After all, if David had gone out to face Goliath only to come back headless on a stretcher, we would not say that David won the battle. So why do Christians speak of the cross as history's greatest instrument of triumph?

Obviously, the resurrection has much to do with that conclusion. But as I noted in this book's introduction, the resurrection alone does not explain why biblical writers speak of the cross *specifically* as a saving conquest. Why, for instance, is it at Christ's death that the veil separating God's presence from God's people is torn in two (Matt. 27:51)? Why is it at Christ's death that he proclaims, "It is finished" (John 19:30)? And why is it specifically at his death that the bodies of several holy people suddenly raised to life like something from *The Walking Dead* (Matt. 27:52–53)? Something special is happening upon the cross that makes it a moment of triumph.[1]

After all, if some other crucifixion victim had miraculously come back to life, ancient people might have inferred all kinds of strange things from the occurrence. But they probably would not have claimed that the victim's *death* had brought about the great defeat of evil. And they certainly would not have assumed they were now forgiven and redeemed because of this extraordinary occurrence.[2]

Yet Scripture claims just that. Colossians states that Jesus disarmed the evil powers and authorities, having "made a public spectacle of them, triumphing over them by the cross" (2:15). To Christians, this line may sound poetic, magnificent, or even familiar, but to any ancient Jew or Roman it would sound downright ridiculous. It's as bizarre as claiming that my friend bested his opponent by getting his own head nearly kicked in and going down by knockout. That brings me back to the central question of this chapter: Why do the New Testament writers refer to the cross *itself* as a victory, a triumph, and a defeat of evil powers?

This third vision of atonement is often called the *Christus victor* theme. That's Latin for "Christ the Victor."[3] The phrase highlights that Jesus saves not merely by (1) re-headshipping humanity, or by (2) bearing the judgment for our sin. Jesus also saves by (3) defeating Satan, death, and evil powers. Salvation comes by conquest. Hence the atonement involves an unexpected victory that allows the Messiah's people—like the Israelites who benefitted from David's defeat of Goliath—to be swept up *in* Christ's triumph so we reign vicariously with our crucified King: *Christus victor!*[4]

Alex and the Donkey God

But don't skip the strangeness. In a culture where crosses adorn our bodies and our buildings, it's easy to forget how grotesque they were. Historian Tom Holland writes: "Only centuries after the death of Jesus did his execution at last start to emerge as an acceptable theme for artists."[5] People who had actually *seen* crosses with screaming, dying, defecating bodies on them were not tempted to emblazon them in 14-karat splendor. Ancient Jews and Romans had witnessed the spikes driven through not only hands and feet but genitals of victims—left to rot on busy streets and highly visible hilltops, completely naked as a further mark of humiliation.[6] No one called these victims "victors."

As I noted in chapter 1, the first drawing we have of Christ's death is a work of graffiti meant to mock the early church. The rude scrawl upon a Roman wall ridiculed a Christian named Alexamenos, who is pictured as a stick figure with his hand raised in reverence. "[Alex] worships his god," proclaims the rough inscription. But as our gaze shifts to the one hanging on the cross, two things stand out about the victim: first, the naked buttocks, and second, the fact that Jesus has been drawn with the head of a donkey. The point behind the sketch is clear: to get crucified by Rome doesn't make you worthy of worship; it makes you an ass.[7]

Why would anyone worship such a god? And why would anyone think this death was a victory?

Isn't that as silly as me looking down at my concussed friend and proclaiming him the winner? The answers to these questions require us to say something about *who* or *what* Christ is said to have defeated by this grotesque instrument. To return to the cage fight analogy, it's time to meet the opponent.

Now Fighting Out of the Red Corner

In chapter 1, I noted that the atonement has layers of meaning because our human predicament has layers too. To put it kindly, humans are a hot mess. We struggle not only with sin and shame and death, we struggle also against evil spiritual powers. So if it isn't strange enough to talk about a crucified victor, we need to bring up Satan too. Scripture clearly views Satan's defeat as a crucial aspect of Christ's saving triumph. In fact, 1 John sums up the reason for Christ's coming with a short statement: "The reason the Son of God appeared was to destroy the devil's work" (3:8b). There you have it.

I once preached a whole sermon on the devil. And though I don't remember much of the content, it must have been effective because, afterward, a woman in the back started hissing, growling, and cursing at another pastor of our church. After this went on for a while, she had to be taken to the hospital. I don't tell that story to make light of the event, and I don't pretend to know what really happened. Was the woman possessed? Did she simply have a mental illness? Or did she just not like that other pastor? I don't know. My point is that

separating demonic activity from mere human brokenness can be challenging

Every few years, Christian polling organizations
release a new survey to show how this next generation
(pick your letter: X, Y, Z, P, that German Ö with the
dots over it) is, in fact, the most secular, unbiblical,
and hell-worthy bunch of youngsters since the youths
who mocked Elijah's bald spot (2 Kings 2:23). Some
of these surveys have value for teaching us about our
friends and neighbors. But others, like so much on the
Internet, are just clickbait. A 2009 study by the Barna
Group garnered lots of Facebook shares by suggesting
that nearly half of Christians surveyed strongly agreed
that the devil is "not a living being but is a symbol
of evil."[8] So although belief in God still ranked high
amongst even nonchurchgoers, the devil had apparently been relegated to the island of unbelievable
creatures, alongside the flying spaghetti monster, the
Easter bunny, and the Super Bowl–winning Detroit
Lions. RIP Satan.

Of course, some views of Satan should be rejected.
In chapter 1, I mentioned segments of the Christian
subculture that hover near the error of making the devil
an equal and opposite power to God. But the opposite
error of smug disbelief has problems too. After all, it
seems odd that so many people would have no trouble
admitting the existence of one spiritual being (God),
but then slam the Overton window on any others.[9]
That's a bit like saying, *Yes, of course, I believe in aliens!
But UFOs are impossible!* This one-and-done approach
to the spirit realm seems odd and inconsistent. In the

face of these extremes regarding the unseen world, the Bible prods us to avoid both *disbelief* and kooky *dualism*. The first excess denies the existence of anything our modern world finds unpalatable, while the second gives Satan too much power.

Why Satan Is a Virus

In Scripture, demonic powers are real but less material and independent than cats and cows and human beings. To understand this point, note how viruses like COVID-19 are not considered to be technically alive or self-sufficient. Viruses steal, kill, and destroy. Yet they require *hosts* to wreak their havoc. Their parasitic power emerges only when they take root and multiply within other life-forms. In fact, a leading theory now (the degeneracy hypothesis) is that RNA viruses represent a devolved and degraded form of living cells that long ago gave up that status to become malignant parasites that stalk the living world. In other words, they fell from a place of original goodness.[10]

There are analogies here that can help us understand evil spiritual powers. Even in the Bible, one rarely meets demons flapping solo about the cosmos. They require hosts to become incarnate.[11] For that reason, the demonic realm (including Satan) is a post-personal category of creatures that were created good by God before devolving and degrading. This is the spiritual equivalent of the degeneracy hypothesis. That conclusion, however, is based not merely on a few proof texts from Scripture,[12] but upon some basic truths about God's character. Namely:

1. God alone is eternal.

2. God alone creates.

3. God is wholly good, so God did not author evil.

4. Nonetheless, evil spiritual powers exist.

5. Thus, evil spiritual powers must have fallen from original goodness.

Put all of this together and you are left with something like the traditional Christian notion of Satan's fall from glory. But none of this means that evil spirits are fully personal, self-sufficient, or alive in the ways that you and I are.[13] Here again the virus analogy helps.

The hosts that evil spirits seek in the Bible are not merely individuals but entire nations, financial systems, and political regimes that get swept up in an antilife agenda that defies logic.[14] Evil is irrational.[15] Thus, these principalities and powers have the ironic characteristic of sometimes sweeping even *themselves* into oblivion. A biblical example of this self-destruction is found in the demons who beg Jesus to send them into some pigs, only to then plunge into the very "Abyss" they sought to avoid by way of this porked-up possession (Luke 8:31–33). As with Jesus on the cross, the destruction of these evil spirits comes precisely by the death of their victim(s) when the demons get the very thing for which they have been scheming.

The result is poetic justice, divine triumph, and a double deathblow.

To return to the viral analogy, an overly aggressive virus may destroy *itself* if it overreaches and kills its host before the pathogen can spread. In this case, the host's death defeats the unseen Enemy because the ravenous parasite inadvertently extinguishes itself in the flesh of its victim. There is a lesson here that points us to Christ's victory. Jesus takes the devil's flaming arrows (Eph. 6:16) into his flesh and he extinguishes their deadly fire with his own blood—*Christus victor!*

"The Fiend Is Overcome"

All this brings me back to Julian of Norwich. In her near-death encounter with Christ (described in chapter 2), Lady Julian had a vision of Jesus on the cross. "In this way," Jesus says regarding his suffering, "the fiend is overcome."[16] The fiend of which Christ speaks is Satan. And to understand why the cross specifically would cause the devil's downfall, we need to move from Satan's nature to his function. To speak of *ha satan* ("the satan" in Hebrew) is not usually to use a personal name like Frank, or Sue, or Javier. Instead, to speak of *ha satan*—the Accuser—is to speak of what the devil does. At the risk of sounding obvious, the Accuser accuses.

Satan appears explicitly just three times in the Old Testament. But each instance shows him acting like a sleazy prosecutor who incites the very crimes he then swoops in to litigate. In this way Satan is akin to an ambulance-chasing attorney who is partly responsible for the very wrongdoings he brings before the judge. Satan incites David to disobey God by taking a census (1 Chron. 21:1). He points out the sinful stains on the garments of the high priest (Zech. 3:1–5). And he accuses Job of only worshipping God because his life is awesome (Job 1–2). There is always a bit of truth in Satan's words, but only that. The end goal is always entrapment and deception.

The same is true in Genesis. Here, the serpent tells Adam and Eve that they will "be like God, knowing good and evil" (Gen. 3:5),[17] and indeed a form of knowledge comes by eating the forbidden fruit. Unfortunately, it is of a shameful kind to which humans would prefer ignorance. This traumatic form of knowledge is like the way you came to know rejection, bullying, or abuse—not by studying the subjects from a distance, but by being swept up in their disturbing wake. Not all knowledge is a blessing.

The partial truthfulness of Satan's accusations highlights *how* Jesus strips the devil of his legal power. Colossians states that Jesus disarmed and overthrew dark spiritual authorities when he "canceled the record of the charges against us . . . by nailing it to the cross" (2:14 NLT). In the Greek language, this legal note of our debt is called the *cheirographon*, but you might think of it as an IOU.[18] In the vivid imagery of Donald MacLeod: "Our guilt, our broken bond, was Satan's title to enslave us and drag us down to hell with himself."[19] The debt owed by covenant-breakers was to undergo the curse of the Law—often exile, or that uber-exile, death.[20]

This penalty highlights the relationship between the Accuser and the judgment due us. As Paul writes: "The wages of sin is death" (Rom. 6:23).

The trouble for all of us apart from Christ is that Satan's accusations have some merit. David really did disobey God's command at great cost. The high priest's robes really were stained metaphorically by sinfulness. And you and I really have sinned grievously in ways that deserve judgment. Thankfully, however, the unscrupulous prosecutor is not the only advocate in the courtroom. Now for the good news.

The Sleazy Lawyer Hurled Out

When I was a young boy, I used to sit with my grandfather and watch *Matlock*.[21] The show was about a folksy, small-town lawyer (played by Andy Griffith) who got his clients acquitted, not merely on some legal technicality, but by revealing the real culprit in dramatic fashion in the courtroom. This move was made even more pleasing by the fact that Matlock did not look like a high-powered, big-city lawyer. He wore the same (cheap) light-gray suit in every episode, often with mustard on the lapel, and he spoke with a molasses-covered drawl. In a word, this advocate seemed *unimpressive*.

So, too, on Calvary. The New Testament refers to both Jesus and the Holy Spirit as our Advocates (John 14:16; 1 John 2:1). The term has many meanings, but one refers to how Christ's work on our behalf has removed the Accuser's legal accusation against us.

In our case, this "not guilty" verdict is not because we've never sinned. It is because the penalty has been paid, the judgment has been carried out, and the prosecutor (Satan) no longer has a case.

Because Jesus took up our humanity (see chapter 2 of this book) and justly bore our judgment (chap. 3), the Accuser's accusations no longer have merit. The book of Hebrews says, "Since the children have flesh and blood, he [Jesus] too shared in their humanity so that by his death he might break the power of him who holds the power of death—that is, the devil" (2:14). That's why Jesus's death on the cross breaks Satan's legal power. The *cheirographon* (Col. 2:14) that signified our debt has been paid in full, so the sleazy lawyer has been hurled out of court. Not even Matlock could orchestrate such an unexpected acquittal!

The book of Revelation makes the same point. There the author hears a loud voice from the throne announcing the good news: God's people have "triumphed" by "the blood of the Lamb" (12:11). Therefore, "the accuser of our brothers and sisters, who accuses them before our God day and night, has been hurled down" (10b).

In sum, Jesus's faithful life and sacrificial blood bring the defeat of Satan because they remove his ability to call for still more judgment on Christ's body—which is us.[22]

This matters for the way you view your past, your present, and your future. Your sin is serious. Make no mistake about it. But you don't have to listen to the accusatory voice when it says you've gone too far to be forgiven. The conviction Satan calls for has *already* been served. And if you give your allegiance to King Jesus, then the Spirit (the other Advocate) now dwells in you—testifying that you are God's beloved child. What's more, this same Spirit is working to transform you on the path of holiness. Satan's enslaving power has been thwarted. That's why Revelation pictures the slain Lamb atop the victor's throne. By his sacrificial death Christ "purchased" with his "blood . . . persons from every tribe and tongue and people and nation" (5:9). The crucifixion drives the nail in Satan's coffin. Hence the cross is spoken of as Christ's instrument of exorcism, through which "the prince of this world will be driven out" (John 12:31).

Where Cross and Kingdom Meet

Of course, Calvary is not the only battlefield in Christ's triumph. One subset of Christians (often, conservative evangelicals) has been so eager to exalt the cross that they sometimes fail to appreciate how every chapter in Christ's story contributes to God's coming kingdom. Meanwhile, another group (often, progressives) have been so quick to emphasize kingdom service—helping widows, orphans, immigrants, and the poor—that they overlook the singular event of the cross as more than just a loving example. As is often the case in our polarized culture, both sides need to be corrected. The kingdom and the cross belong together. For as Jeremy Treat argues: "The kingdom is the ultimate goal of the cross, and the cross is the means by which the kingdom comes."[23]

There's a reason Jesus's saving death did not take place just after his birth, when the wicked King Herod was killing Jewish babies (Matt. 2:16). For while the cross stands at the center of gospel preaching (1 Cor. 2:2), it does not stand alone—as if all the important parts of redemption have been covered in the Apostles' Creed, when it skips from Jesus being "born of the Virgin Mary" to "suffered under Pontius Pilate." The stuff in the middle matters too.[24] Long before the empty tomb, Christ's work was couched in terms of a kingdom-building conquest.

In psychedelic fashion, the book of Revelation pictures Jesus's birth as a scene of apocalyptic combat. There's even a seven-headed dragon (Satan) waiting to devour the Christ-child, only to have the baby snatched away to safety (Rev. 12:1–6). From this vantage point, Christmas is less a silent sentimental night, and more a violent cosmic contest.[25]

The war continues in Jesus's public ministry. Christ's obedience in the face of wilderness temptation is a triumph that contrasts with the failures of both Adam and Israel. His healings reveal a Holy One who is eradicating the forces of death even while he lived.[26] And his casting out of demons shows him driving the Evil One from his stronghold not just in creation, but in the human body itself. To be Israel's Messiah was not just to make religious claims about God, morality, and salvation, it was to fight the ultimate cage fight against

Israel's true Enemy: not merely Babylon or Rome, but Satan himself.

Each page of the Gospels tells the *Christus victor* story in multiple dimensions. Yet at each turn the victories are paradoxical. Jesus is clearly pictured as the great Davidic king, the long-awaited Messiah who will restore God's suffering people. Yet he is most like David not in the bloody beatdown of his foes,[27] but in a kingship marked by tears, abandonment, allegations of insanity,[28] and ultimately a raspy cry from the cross that is a quote from Israel's suffering psalmist: "My God, my God, why have you forsaken me?" (Ps. 22:1; Matt. 27:46).[29]

But the story doesn't end there. Easter also sings the song of *Christus victor*. After all, few moves carry more swagger than the ability to mount a comeback over death, walk boldly from a borrowed tomb, and live forever in a body that no longer experiences the results of human fallenness. Old Alexamenos really would have been a fool if his Lord had simply remained there dead upon on the cross. Without the resurrection, our faith would be futile, and we would still be stuck in our sins (1 Cor. 15:17). Thankfully, both the empty tomb and Christ's ascension to the throne of heaven chant a common chorus: *Christus victor!*

Conclusion

So far in this book I've shown how different aspects of Christ's saving work fit together. Let's review: The radical nature of the solution reveals the true depths of our predicament (chap. 1). But because Jesus is the true Adam and true Israel, he can faithfully represent us (chap. 2) and even bear the judgment we deserved (chap. 3). That's why the cross becomes an instrument of victory: Sin's debt has been paid and Satan's accusations no longer have power over us (chap. 4).

Jesus saves because he triumphs over death and the devil. Yet he does so in the most surprising way: He wins by losing. He conquers by his own knockout. And his cross becomes the wood for a King's throne. Yet this strange victory is not some bit of metaphorical nonsense. It is not the same as me leaning over my concussed friend at the cage fight and saying, "Good news, man; you won!" Christ's victory is real. In fact, it was foretold as far back as Genesis 3. There we find the "first gospel"—the *protoevangelium*. God tells Adam and Eve that the woman's offspring will one day crush the serpent's head, even as the deadly serpent simultaneously strikes the servant's "heel" (Gen. 3:15). The prophesy is of a double deathblow, a conquest that involves the victor's fatal piercing. That strange triumph happens on the cross, and in every moment of Christ's ministry. Now it's time to see how we ourselves can be transformed by this kingdom-building victory.

ENGAGE THE TEXT

To reflect on Jesus's saving victory, read the following passages and ask God to speak to you about atonement as a strange triumph:

- Genesis 3:14–15
- Psalm 2 and Psalm 9
- Colossians 2:13–15
- 1 John 3:7–8

DISCUSS THE TEXT

1. This chapter reflects on Christ's saving defeat of death and the devil. But it began by acknowledging the strangeness of that mode of conquest: death on a cross.

    - Why is it good news that our victorious Messiah experienced defeat in the most shameful way? How does that fact encourage you?
    - Do you think the symbol of the cross has lost its meaning and strangeness today? Why or why not?
    - How might you recover the scandal of the cross in your own life and family?

2. One enemy that Christ defeated is the devil.

    - How did the translation of *ha satan* (the Accuser) not as a name but as a function shed light on Satan's work in our world?

- How has the voice of the Accuser come to you?
- Have you had any experiences with what you would call the demonic?

3. Christ defeats Satan by removing the ground of his accusation, by taking the full penalty for sin upon himself.

   - How does this chapter, about victory, stand upon the foundation of the prior chapters: re-headshipping (chap. 2) and penalty-bearing (chap. 3)?

4. At the end of the chapter, the author wrote the following:

   > One subset of Christians (often, conservative evangelicals) has been so eager to exalt the cross that they sometimes fail to appreciate how every chapter in Christ's story contributes to God's coming kingdom. Meanwhile, another group (often, progressives) have been so quick to emphasize kingdom service—helping widows, orphans, immigrants, and the poor—that they overlook the singular event of the cross as more than just a loving example. As is often the case in our polarized culture, both sides need to be corrected.

   - Which extreme have you been more prone toward? And what would it look like to adopt a more balanced and biblical perspective?

Chapter Five

Jesus and Severus Snape

Always." The millions of readers who have completed J. K. Rowling's Harry Potter saga know the meaning of that one-word refrain. It is the response of Severus Snape—the grim and apparently vindictive Hogwarts professor—when asked if he *still* loves Lily Potter. She was the kindhearted girl who stole his heart when he was just an oily and awkward young boy. Snape's transformation is the most beloved aspect of the Harry Potter series, as evidenced by the online forums which consistently rank him (above even Harry) as the favorite character. But it didn't start that way.

Through most of the books, we are led to believe that Snape is at best a bitter and malevolent teacher. He despises Harry for unknown reasons. And at worst, he seems like a murderous turncoat who does the bidding of Lord Voldemort. In fact, Snape—like most of us—is complicated. Yet by the end he turns out to be one of the story's greatest heroes, giving up his life to save others, and prompting Harry to say, "He was probably the bravest man I ever knew."[1] What caused this transformation? In a word, it was an experience of redemptive *love*.

Love Is Our Religion

Love is everyone's religion. It is not merely the domain of reckless romantics who tear off each other's clothes in fits of passion. Nor is it the sole possession of those poor sops who kneel before the altar of Nicholas Sparks. In the view of Saint Augustine, every person acts in accordance with their greatest loves. "My weight is my love," he says in a passage that likens longing to a force of gravity. "Wherever I am carried, my love is carrying me."[2] And this directing weight, when it gets heavy enough, will even bring you to your knees—not necessarily in a marriage proposal, but in worship.

A key difference in our respective religions is where we *aim* our deepest desires: toward a six-figure salary, a smaller waist size, a larger church, an eldest child, a romantic partner, or more likely—at the person in the mirror. As with Professor Snape, love always transforms us. But that transformation is not always for the better. We are molded into the image of the things we chase most passionately. We resemble what we most revere.[3] Thus the Christian philosopher James K. A. Smith, writes: "You are what you love." Unfortunately, "You might not love what you think."[4] Here, too, we are like the Hogwarts potions master: our true affections and allegiances often fly under the radar, not only from our friends and colleagues, but from ourselves. Like Snape, we're complicated.

By now you're probably wondering: *What does all this love-talk have to do with how Jesus saves?* Glad you asked. There is a fourth and final atonement explanation that focuses upon the transforming power of God's love. It's often called the "moral influence" model. But the title is misleading. It makes this model sound like little more than a nudge toward ethical behavior—like when I exert a moral influence on my children by telling them to clean their rooms or stop pestering a cat. In fact, this answer to how Jesus saves focuses on the way Christ's sacrificial love enflames our hearts to endure anything for him, not out of fear or guilt, but out of gratitude: "Always." Now let's unpack the history of this model of salvation.

The Emasculated Monk

It starts, by some accounts, with a medieval genius-monk who seduced a bright young maiden named Heloise, conceived a child with her out of wedlock, married her in secret, penned the most famous love letters of his millennium, and was then brutally castrated when her angry uncle hired thugs to punish him for the torrid affair.[5] (Yes, all that is true.) The monk's name was Peter Abelard. And aside from a bio that sounds like a salacious HBO drama—probably starring someone with bigger muscles and a smaller brain than Abelard himself—he was also arguably the greatest philosopher-theologian of his age.[6]

Despite ultimately affirming several biblical models of atonement, Abelard's romantic heart returned most frequently to the transformative power of an act of love, performed for those who don't deserve it. In reflecting on the book of Romans, he spoke of how Jesus bound us to himself by love, taught love by word and deed, poured love into our hearts by the Holy Spirit (Rom. 5:5), and thus ignited our love-response of grateful obedience.[7] For Abelard, the atonement was a love story from start to finish. And in this point, he was merely echoing something said far earlier by Augustine: "What greater cause is there of the Lord's coming than to show God's love for us?"[8]

Unfortunately, some people took Abelard as saying that Jesus saved us *only* by his loving example, as if all we needed was a role model instead of a rescue from sin, death, and the devil. In the twelfth century, Saint Bernard (the person, not the giant canine) wrote a letter to the Pope in which he branded Abelard a heretic for espousing this "good example" view of salvation.[9] Bernard lambasted the emasculated monk with sarcasm by suggesting that if Jesus only saved us by a display of good deeds, maybe Adam only harmed us by a "display" of eating an apple.[10] It was a deep cut, but almost as unfair to Abelard as was Heloise's angry uncle.

In time, however, some Christians (in progressive circles especially) did see Christ's saving work *merely* as a powerful example. This more exclusive form of the moral influence model is often called exemplarism. Its idea is that when we see how much Christ loved us, our callous hearts are pierced by saving gratitude and we are drawn *to God* like metal to a massive magnet.[11]

The problem to be overcome in this view of salvation is not something outside of us—say, God's judgment or Satan's affliction—but our *own* refusal to approach our gracious Savior and imitate his character. Jesus's loving example supposedly shatters that fearful or apathetic attitude within us.

This stripped-down view of salvation has been popular in a secular culture that is willing to see Jesus as a great teacher, but not as the saving sacrifice for sin. After all, to accept it as the only explanation of how Jesus saves means you can discard many traditional bits of the atonement: divine judgment, the divinity of Christ, and the existence of the devil. But is this *good example* view actually good news? In my view, Bernard was right to scorn the notion that we may be saved merely by a display of sacrificial love, even though he was wrong to locate this opinion within the work of Abelard himself. Let me explain.

A Day at the Beach

I've always been a bad swimmer. While others seem to float effortlessly on their backs or glide smoothly across the pool, I have sometimes said that "I can't swim to save my life." But that's not true. I can swim a little bit, if only for short distances and with the grace and poise of a person being attacked by a swarm of angry bees. What I *can't* do is swim to save the life of someone else. And that inability (along with some poor parenting on my part) led to the most frightening experience of my life.

This past summer, my family was enjoying a beach day at our usual vacation spot in Florida. Two of my children, Penelope and Ewan, were wading in what had been waist-deep water. I was reading a book. My wife had just left briefly to go up to the house, which meant I was in charge. Somehow, between glances up from my book, a rogue wave came and swept my six-year-old son (who cannot swim) into a powerful rip current. When my daughter Penelope screamed, "Dad, Ewan!" I looked up to see every parent's nightmare: their small child dragged out into the ocean, with his head periodically disappearing beneath the choppy waves. I tore into the water, cutting my feet and knees on the coquina rocks, and shouting "Help!" at the top of my lungs.

The worst feeling in that moment was the realization that I probably could not save him. I had to try, of course. But as I struggled out toward him, I couldn't suppress the dread that we might both be drowned as my other three kids stood watching. Miraculously, two men who happened to hear my screams came charging into the water, more gracefully than me. They made it to my son before I did. And it took all their effort to haul him in. Somehow, we all made it. And between my gasps for air, I thanked the men who saved my son at the risk of their own safety.

I tell that story because it reminds me of an illustration about the moral influence model of how Jesus saves. It was told years ago by Scottish preacher James Denney.[12] Denney asked his audience to imagine themselves happily sunbathing at the end of a long pier. (Go ahead; see if you can do it after my tale of beachside terror.) As you are enjoying your book, suddenly a man races past you on the pier, jumps over the railing, and begins to drown in the surf. "I'm doing this because I love you!" he splutters back at you, before slipping finally beneath the waves to his death. Cute story, huh?

The complete lack of good news in the odd tale is precisely Denney's point. It is neither loving nor saving for a man to die *solely* to display how much he cares. Unnecessary acts of self-harm are closer to manipulation than saving grace. Consider the troubled artist, van Gogh, who reportedly cut off his own ear and presented the bloody appendage, wrapped in a cloth, to a prostitute at the local brothel. "I'm doing this because I love you!" he might have written next to a little drawing with some swirly clouds. The picture might be priceless, but the severed ear is gross. The reason is simple: unbidden acts of self-harm which are designed to generate a response are not actually a good example, and they are not good news.

Now consider a different version of Denney's sunbathing analogy. Imagine (as Denney suggests) that *you* are the one drowning in that churning ocean, having brought about your fate by foolishness and pride and maybe some poor parenting. Then imagine that a man jumps off the pier and saves you at the cost of his own life. Now *that*'s an act of saving love—and it could spark a life-altering gratitude. Unlike the first example, the death of this rescuer actually accomplishes something salvific. Thus we would say with

Denney and with Christ himself, "Greater love has no one than this: to lay down one's life for one's friends" (John 15:13).[13]

I'm grateful that this didn't happen to me or to the men that rescued my drowning son. But Scripture teaches that it *did* happen when Jesus laid down his life not just for friends or strangers, but for enemies. What's more, many noble humans have offered up their lives for others, but only one person (the God-man) could truly deal with sin, break the power of death, and overcome the devil. That's why 1 John proclaims: "This is love: not that we loved God, but that he loved us and sent his Son as an atoning sacrifice for our sins" (4:10).[14]

Transformed, Not Just Acquitted

Unfortunately, since this so-called "moral influence" view cannot explain the whole of redemption, some Christians have downplayed it entirely. The sad result, in many sermons and youth camp altar calls, is that the whole emphasis is placed upon how Jesus took your penalty, averted divine judgment, or conquered death so you could live forever. These ideas are true. And they are glorious. But they are not sufficient. The reason is that God is not interested in merely removing sin's penalty; he's also heaven-bent on freeing you from sin's power. Jesus's work is about transformation, not just acquittal.

To emphasize *only* my forgiveness or my escape from hell is a selfish view of atonement. Yet in the Bible, the good news is about God and his coming kingdom. Atonement is also about the establishment of God's reign on earth, as it is in heaven—which is another reason we can't just skip past the moral influence model. The transformative power of God's love should not be treated like a shamefully neglected stepchild, plopped down next to the real models of atonement in an awkward family photo.

Romans 16:20 Says

For some biblical proof, consider one of the most annoying youth camp songs of all time: "ROMANS 16:19 SAYS!" (It must be written in all caps or Chris Tomlin will show up at your house to key your car.) If you're a child of the '90s, you may remember moshing to this anthem while a sweaty worship leader beat his Taylor guitar as if it said something despicable about his mother. But despite its merits as a song that doubled as a Bible memory verse, the reference to Romans 16:19 is inaccurate. Because more than half the lyrics come from Romans 16:20.[15]

In Paul's letter, Romans 16:19 follows a discussion about transformed lives that Christians are to lead—lives of wisdom, obedience, unity, and humble service. Then Paul informs his readers: "The God of peace will soon crush Satan under your feet" (v. 20). This verse is Paul's nod to Genesis 3:15, a passage we discussed at the end of the last chapter. The promise there was that the offspring of the woman would crush the head of the satanic serpent. That crushing is what we termed a "double deathblow" (chap. 4) since the same heel that does the stomping is simultaneously pierced by the serpent's poisonous fangs. One might say the piercing made the stomping possible—since (and now I'm speaking of the cross) Christ's wounds were the means by which the devil was "nailed down" when Jesus bore our judgment. For all these reasons, Genesis 3:15 has incredible poetic and prophetic power.

Yet notice how Paul tweaks this verse from Genesis. Whose feet are doing the stomping in Romans 16:20? We would expect Paul to say that the God of peace will soon crush Satan underneath Christ's foot or, perhaps, under the heel of the Messiah. But he doesn't. Paul proclaims that the God of peace will soon crush Satan "under your feet."[16] Was the apostle playing loose with Scripture? Was he taking the emphasis off Christ's victory and placing it on your natural Satan-stomping potential? Not at all.

Paul's great revelation, back on the Damascus Road, was that followers of Jesus are the body of Christ on earth.[17] So while we wrongly think of ourselves as disconnected and autonomous individuals, Paul conceives of us as the eyes and arms and stomping feet of the Messiah. That's why the Bible scholar G. B. Caird says the moral transformation of sinners into saints constitutes the defeat of evil power.[18] That transformation—*your transformation*—into a new person, with new habits and priorities, is connected to the stomping of the devil's head, both now and in the future.

That's why this moral influence model of atonement is not just an unnecessary add-on to God's past work of reconciliation. There is also a present and ongoing aspect to atonement. And here again we see why the kingdom and the cross cannot be separated. Paul writes elsewhere that the same God who has "reconciled us to himself though Christ" has also given us "the ministry of reconciliation" (2 Cor. 5:18). But if we are going to grasp how terribly imperfect people like ourselves can become participants in God's reconciling work, we're going to need to say something about a sometimes-forgotten member of the Trinity.

The Spirit of Atonement

Atonement is often called the work of Christ—and rightly so. But Jesus never acts alone to save us. He does everything in harmonious union with the Father and the Holy Spirit: one God, three persons [19] We've already spoken a fair bit about the Father in the chapter that dealt with Jesus taking on our penalty (chap. 3).[20] But we have yet to say much about the Holy Spirit. It's time to remedy that silence.

The Spirit is active in every model of atonement. So we shouldn't relegate the Holy Spirit's importance to *only* the moral influence theme.[21] Consider our first atonement model in which Jesus faithfully re-headships humanity as the new and true Adam (chap. 2): Christ is conceived by "the Holy Spirit" (Matt. 1:20); hence his act of assuming our humanity is the fruit of the Spirit's work. Christ is also filled and led by the Spirit, so he acts faithfully on our behalf, instead of failing like Adam did. Christ lives this faultless life not by periodically tapping in to his divine nature like a latent superpower, but by dependence on the Spirit's help.

Moving next to Jesus bearing our judgment (chap. 3), the Spirit is likewise essential. The justice of Christ's penalty-bearing (one person for others) only makes sense if we are bound up *in* our Messiah. That union is the product of the Spirit's work even as it is rooted in Christ's identity as the perfect Image of God, after whom humanity was patterned. Finally, when we speak of salvation as a triumph over death and the devil (chap. 4), we find that the Spirit is the means of war against the forces of darkness. (We call it *spirit*ual warfare after all [Matt. 12:28].) And the Spirit joins the Father as the agent not merely of Christ's conception, but of his triumphant resurrection.

Now here's more good news: If you've given your allegiance to King Jesus, the same Spirit that raised Christ from the dead now dwells in you (Rom. 8:10–11). That Spirit will produce in you what Paul calls the Spirit's fruit: love, joy, peace, patience, kindness, goodness, faithfulness, gentleness, and self-control (Gal. 5:22–23). This bundle of attributes is precisely the "moral influence" that the moral influence model of atonement is all about. The Spirit produces this fruit, and it amounts to a transformed character which contributes to a transformed world.

The Dead End of Authenticity

I'm not saying this transformation will be quick or easy. Nor will it be perfectly complete within this life.

But your transformation by the Spirit's moral influence does stand distinct from the two contrasting views of personal renewal on the table in modern culture.

The first of these views is what we might call the Path of Authenticity. You find it in a plethora of self-care and self-esteem literature, often marketed to so-called wine moms, but sometimes sold to men as well. The Path of Authenticity is all about how you need to stop apologizing for being you, stop conforming to others people's expectations, and simply lean in to *your* authentic, untamed, inner, primal, fierce, free, fire, goddess, warrior, lover self. "YOU ARE ENOUGH," is the tagline of this burgeoning industry of books, podcasts, and branded novelty T-shirts. Behold: the Path of Authenticity.

Now. Before you throw my book across the room for mocking a legion of beleaguered wine moms who are just trying to make it through the day between toddler meltdowns, preteen soccer practices, postpartum depression, and emotionally inept husbands, let me say: There is a grain of truth along the Path of Authenticity. You are loved just as you are, and you should move toward honesty and authenticity. By all means, wash your face (if you want), and stop apologizing for things you haven't done wrong. But despite all these helpful points, the Path of Authenticity omits two massive biblical truths that are required for a satisfying life: You are not your own, and you are not enough.[22]

The Path of Authenticity is self-focused, as some of its proponents openly admit.[23] It assumes that if you just dig deeply and honestly inside your psyche, you will find a "true self." And this true self will provide the infallible compass by which to live. But frankly, if I could be so honest, that's nonsense. You know it's nonsense because you have spent time with your "true self"—and you know that he or she is an unreliable narrator.

Scripture says humans were created good, but are all now terribly fallen. And it's not just the outward, inauthentic, socially repressed "you" that is fallen. Your "true self" is fallen too (Jer. 17:9). Yes, you do many kind and beautiful things. But there is no untrammeled, uncorrupted inner self to be unearthed within your tangled web of emotions, experiences, and indigestion. Your authentic self might be a narcissistic jerk. But even if it's just mildly annoying, leaning in to "the real you" for fulfillment is a bad move. It could easily end your marriage, make you insufferable on social media, or cause you to waste tons of money on hastily constructed, mass-marketed, (probably) ghost-written books that are mistakenly housed within the "Christian living" category. You are *not* enough. That's actually the problem that necessitated Christ's atoning work. You need a Savior. The Path of Authenticity is a dead end.

The Dead End of Self-Improvement

But if the Path of Authenticity is a false road, so, too, is its opposite: the Path of Self-Improvement. While the former urges you to recover your true self (which is *already* unfallen, sufficient, and whole), the latter says it's possible to *become* what you're now not through discipline, hard work, and, of course, the products that you will need to complete your transformation.

If the Path of Authenticity preys upon some stereotypical feminine dispositions, then the Path of Self-Improvement (or "self authoring"[24]) often cashes in on the masculine hubris that I can pull myself up by the bootstraps, exert some grit, and transform myself into the person I'd like to be. This may be done by hard work, twelve (or more) rules for life, and a steady diet of *The Joe Rogan Experience*. The thing is, you probably can't. Yes, you can certainly clean your room, be a more responsible employee, and maybe even add fifty pounds to your back squat. You *can* improve those outward aspects of your life. And you should. (Unless you have bad knees.) But those outward accomplishments will not renew your heart or soul. And anyway, Christians don't believe we are saved by becoming really enthusiastic, community minded, muscle-bound individuals. That's not the gospel; that's CrossFit.

Another Helper

The trouble with both the Path of Authenticity and the Path of Self-Improvement is they often share a common, broken core: Despite some good qualities, both paths communicate that *you* (the sovereign individual) are king. You belong to you. And since you belong to you, you alone are responsible for your transformation into the hero of your story.[25]

But that's not how it works in Scripture. Heck, that's not even how it works in Harry Potter. Snape wasn't transformed by self-love or self-improvement. He couldn't just stare into a magic mirror and utter "You are enough!" till he believed it. You'd throw that story across the room for being both ridiculous and boring. Snape needed Lily Potter to save him, if only as she lived on as a silver thread within his memory.

The Bible speaks of the Holy Spirit as the Helper or Advocate who lives within us. But this indwelling is much more than a mere recollection. "If you love me," Jesus says, "keep my commands. And I will ask the Father, and he will give you another advocate to help you and be with you forever—the Spirit of truth" (John 14:15–17a). Jesus continues:

> "The world cannot accept him, because it neither sees him nor knows him. But you know him, for he lives with you and will be in you. I will not leave you as orphans; I will come to you. . . .
>
> "All this I have spoken while still with you. But the Advocate, the Holy Spirit, whom the Father will send in my name, will teach you all things and will remind you of everything I have said to you. Peace I leave with you; my peace I give you. I do not give to you as the world gives. Do not let your hearts be troubled and do not be afraid." (John 14:17b–18, 25–27)

The Holy Spirit inside us is the engine of transformation. The Spirit causes us to view God not as a mysterious or cruel taskmaster, but as *Abba*—the perfect Father we cry out to when we don't know what to say (Rom. 8:26). The Spirit convicts us of sin when we'd like to sweep it under the rug, or attribute it to our authentic self (John 16:8). The Spirit frees up our broken wills so we can exercise a kind of freedom that makes us neither puppets nor autonomous individuals (1 Cor. 12:3; 2 Cor. 3:17).[26]

The Spirit illuminates God's written Word (the Bible) so we are not left completely to the woo-woo whims of mysticism. The Spirit fuses personal morality with a concern for justice in the world. Because after all, as Cornell West notes, justice is simply what love looks like in public.[27] The Spirit infuses our singing with enthusiasm, so our bodies and our souls are reunited, instead of leaving us like dour statues.

The Spirit is the bringer of a unity that is not uniformity, so that persons of all races, nationalities, and (yes) political backgrounds are knit together in a messy but mutually submissive family. The Spirit sends us out on mission, just as on that first Pentecost (Acts 2), when unschooled fishermen proclaimed the gospel with no concern for outward appearance, established credentials, or hickish accents. The Spirit also blows afresh with signs and wonders even today— not as a kind of automatic, formulaic guarantee based on doubt-free faith or monetary contribution—but as a reminder that the same God who parted waters, conquered armies, cast out demons, raised up the dead, and filled both barren wombs and empty wine glasses is *still* in the miracle business. He is an old, strong God. He is not held captive by the laws of physics that he wrote.

This same Spirit, as the prophet Joel proclaimed, is poured out in these last days on all flesh, male *and* female. So not only sons but also daughters prophesy. By the Spirit's outpouring, not only men but also women step in to their empowered callings, alongside past leaders of God's people like Deborah, Huldah, Phoebe, Junia, Priscilla, and the prophetic daughters of Philip. This same Spirit causes the elderly to dream new dreams while the young receive a vision of a different future (Joel 2:28–29). Finally, the Spirit joins the bride—which is the church—in saying "Come!" Come quickly, Lord Jesus, to the world you love, to the world you died to save, and to the world bought back from bondage by your blood (Rev. 22:17, 20).

I get amped up to write of such bold prospects. But a crucial caveat is needed. Spirit-birthed hope is not the same as breezy optimism. Make no mistake: *You and everyone you love will die.* Your kids. Your spouse. Your dearest friends. Despite the Spirit's regenerating work, dark and terrible days will still befall you. But amid this sobering reminder, take heart: The same Paul who met the risen Jesus, was filled by his Spirit, worked miracles, and authored much of the New Testament also weathered horrific bouts of depression, and what we might call a mental breakdown. What's more, these hard times were not relegated to Paul's pre-Christian life before he was filled with Jesus's Spirit:

> We do not want you to be uninformed, brothers
> and sisters, about the troubles we experienced
> in the province of Asia. We were under great

pressure, far beyond our ability to endure, so that we despaired of life itself. Indeed, we felt we had received the sentence of death. But this happened that we might not rely on ourselves but on God, who raises the dead. (2 Cor. 1:8–9)

This, too, is the Spirit's work—helping us endure the sentence of death without succumbing to despair.[28] Which reminds me, we shouldn't end this chapter without returning to a final lesson from the love story of Severus Snape.

Why Guilt Is Not Enough

Toward the end of *The Deathly Hallows*, Harry finally learns the truth about his least favorite Hogwarts teacher.[29] He learns that Snape was driven all these years not merely by a love for Lily, nor solely by a hatred for Harry's father, but by the shame of knowing that his sins contributed to Lily's death. His heroic and conflicting actions were compelled not merely by love, but by a crushing guilt.

Guilt trips often serve as motivators. After all, guilt can be a powerful moral influence. By way of example, my wife recalls the sermon that first led her to make a public commitment to Christ. The preacher went on and on, in excruciating detail, about the agony that Christ experienced upon the cross—the medical details, the blood and gore, and all with a flourish at the end: "You did that! *Your* sin! Now quit hitting your sister." (Okay, I added that last part.)

Of course, there is a degree to which that's true. Human sin did bring about Christ's suffering, and we each add to that collective pile of evil. But we must be careful lest we craft a Snape-like model of redemption rather than the biblical one. Scripture actually avoids turning the cross into an R-rated meditation upon the most macabre aspects of Jesus's torture and death.[30] That's because the point was never psychological manipulation by a prolonged guilt trip. Being pricked with guilt can cause us to repent and run to Christ. But guilt is not a healthy long-term motivator.

Ask Severus Snape. He is tortured and miserable even as he undertakes heroic actions. Just look at him. He needs a counselor, a vacation, and definitely a new shampoo. He might do noble things after experiencing the weight of his misdeeds, but he's doing it, at least partly, to atone for what he did. Some Christians are that way as well.

The final lesson of Christ's transforming, Spirit-enabled act of grace is that it is motivated more by gratitude than guilt. That's why Jesus doesn't spend his post-resurrection time going on and on to the disciples about how bad they should feel for having killed him by their sins. "And when I died, I saw your face!" is never uttered by the real Jesus. What he asks, even to Peter who denied him three times, is not "Do you feel sufficiently terrible?" but rather, "Do you love me?" (John 21:17). Only love can motivate Peter to do the hard things he will be called to do. *His weight is his love.* As is yours. So in this regard we should follow Augustine, Abelard, and Scripture rather than

the sorcerer, Severus Snape. (And with that, the anti–
Harry Potter homeschooler moms can breathe a sigh
of relief.)

By the Spirit's power, the moral influence model
of atonement shows how Christ's radical and sacrificial love enflames our hearts to endure anything
for him—not out of fear or guilt, but out of loving
gratitude—"Always."

ENGAGE THE TEXT

To reflect on the saving power of Christ's love, read the following passages and ask God to speak to you about how Christ's example might transform you by the power of the Holy Spirit:

- John 3:16–18
- John 15:9–17
- 1 Corinthians 13
- 1 John 4:7–21

DISCUSS THE TEXT

1. This chapter began with a bold claim: "Love is everyone's religion."

   > A key difference in our respective religions is where we aim our deepest desires: toward a six-figure salary, a smaller waist size, a larger church, an eldest child, a romantic partner, or more likely—at the person in the mirror.

   - Do you agree with this claim? What key figure from the early church (fourth century) bolstered it?
   - Take an inventory of your own life. What object, person, or activity is most likely to take preeminence over God as your ultimate priority?
   - What kinds of habits or beliefs might be required to keep that object or person in the

proper place in your affections—as good, but not ultimate?

2. Although Peter Abelard did not view the cross as *only* an inspiring example, why do you think so many people want to see Jesus as a good role model, but not the one and only rescuer of humanity?

   • How did the author's example of a "day at the beach" speak to the problem of viewing the cross as nothing more than a demonstration of love?
   • Why is it important that this moral influence model of atonement sits atop the foundation laid in the prior chapters?

3. While some progressive Christians have downplayed the cross as an objective payment of sin's penalty, or a defeat of Satan, many more conservative Christians have downplayed the moral influence model of atonement.

   • Why is important that we be transformed and not just acquitted?
   • How does a proper view of the moral influence model place a proper focus on the cross and the kingdom-lifestyle launched by Christ?
   • Why is the Holy Spirit crucially important as the engine of our transformation?

4. The end of the chapter detailed two dead ends: the Path of Authenticity and the Path of Self-Improvement.

- How would you define each path?
- Which are you more prone toward, and why?
- Despite their strengths, why are each of these paths dead ends, compared to the good news of God's saving love?

CONCLUSION

UNIVERSAL DONOR

Apparently, I have rare blood. Not long ago, I came across a friend's heartfelt Facebook post about a little girl named Hattie. She was clinging to life in a children's hospital and in dire need of platelets. Unfortunately, because of Hattie's blood type, and the terrible toll of the COVID-19 pandemic, her city no longer had many platelets left to give her. The call went out: Does anyone have AB negative blood? As it turns out, I do. This rare blood is found in less than one percent of humans. And it is especially valuable because those who have it function as universal donors of platelets and plasma to people like Hattie. Of course, I began making calls to see if I could help.

The atonement also is about a universal donor. It is a story of rare blood. And this blood is offered not only for the good people—the beautiful, the successful, and those with all the right opinions—but for every single sinner who has ever lived. That's why a former persecutor like the apostle Paul can say that "Christ died for the ungodly" (Rom. 5:6). What's more, this donation was not random or impersonal. Paul says elsewhere that the Son of God "loved *me* and gave himself for *me*" (Gal. 2:20, emphasis added). That's how Jesus saves—with radical, universal, yet deeply personal love.

Based on my young daughter's bedtime question, this book has looked at several historic models of atonement. We tackled questions and objections. And we asked how reconciliation could possibly come by the violent, grotesque, and apparently tragic means of a Roman cross. Those are dense discussions. But we tried to frame them in words and images that are accessible for ordinary people—since that's who Jesus came to save. Let's review one last time.

The true diagnosis. First, we saw how the cross reveals the true extent of our collective human problem. Like a cosmic CAT scan, Christ comes not just to heal but also to diagnose our ailments. The objection handled in this chapter was: "Why do I need atonement?" And in answering it, my claim was that we don't simply need some good advice, a good role model, a new guru, a fresh word of self-esteem, or a swift kick in the backside. We need a Savior to redeem God's good-but-broken creation—because our problems are both numerous and serious.

The true Adam. Second, we saw how Jesus saves us as the true Adam who took up our humanity and relived the human drama faithfully on our behalf (chap. 2). The key question tackled here was: "How can one person act for all the others?" Against modern individualism, we found that the Bible stresses the cosmic bound-togetherness of all things in the Son of God, the true Image of the invisible God. In the Bible, the head can act for the whole. That's why atonement happens not just in the moment of Christ's death, but through his—big word alert!—recapitulative life.[1]

The true sacrifice. Third, Jesus saves by willingly bearing the judgment for the sins of the whole world (chap. 3). The objection here was: "How can an innocent person die for the guilty?" The answer involved Jesus's identity as the head of humanity, and the one person in whom all things are bound together. Far from being abusive against the weak and vulnerable, Christ's judgment-bearing death reveals a mighty God who becomes weak and poor for others (Phil. 2:6–8). The all-powerful one enters human brokenness, identifies with victims, and repudiates the myth that power must be wielded exploitatively. Thus, Christ's act of taking up our judgment is not the upending of biblical justice, it is its heart and soul.

The true victor. Fourth, we saw how Christ's penalty bearing death brings about his victory over death and the devil. The question answered in this chapter was a big one: "Why view the cross as a triumph?" In response, we found that because sin's judgment has been borne, the devil's accusations no longer have the final word over those who belong to Christ. That's why the book of Hebrews celebrates the fact that Christ "shared in [our] humanity so that by his death he might break the power of him who holds the power of death—that is, the devil" (2:14). The fact that Jesus conquers by humble obedience and sacrificial love also shows how we shall overcome—not by adopting the world's power plays and tactics (the way of the Dragon), but by the way of the victorious Lamb.

The true act of love. Finally, we explored how the cross reveals God's transforming love (chap. 5). This so-called moral influence model builds upon the others even as it taps into a fundamental truth that governs your behavior: You are not driven primarily by what you think, by what you believe, or by what you have been told to do. You are driven by your deepest loves.[2] Thankfully, Christ's transforming love is more than just a good example. Jesus accomplishes objective things on our behalf (chaps. 1–4). And the engine behind the moral influence model is God himself—specifically, God the Holy Spirit.

Redemption is not a kind of crude transaction that occurs merely between the Father and the Son, Christ and Satan, or even God and humanity. Atonement is also the fruit of the Spirit working to make us new from the inside out. The Spirit awakens us to Christ, frees our fallen wills, unites us to Jesus, leads us on the path of holiness, and then blows afresh across our groaning world as we await in hope for God's new creation.

NOTES

Introduction: Atonement for Ordinary People

1. Joshua M. McNall, *The Mosaic of Atonement: An Integrated Approach to Christ's Work* (Grand Rapids: Zondervan Academic, 2019).
2. I steal this point (minus the Elvis and Tupac reference) from N. T. Wright. Wright asks us to consider what made Christ's resurrection more meaningful than if one of the two criminals crucified alongside him had somehow been raised again.
3. For a brief treatment of resurrection and atonement, see my blog post, "Raised for Our Justification," May 10, 2021, at https://joshuamcnall.com/2021/05/10/raised-for-our-justification/.
4. Alan Noble, *Disruptive Witness: Speaking Truth in a Distracted Age* (Downers Grove, IL: IVP, 2018), 3.
5. Andrew Sullivan, "I Used to Be a Human Being," *New York Magazine*, September 19, 2016. https://nymag.com/intelligencer/2016/09/andrew-sullivan-my-distraction-sickness-and-yours.html.

Chapter One: Jesus and the Bigger Boat

1. The Bible teaches that some calamities (for instance, the fall of Jerusalem in 586 BC) served as punishments on human idolatry, evil, and oppression. Still, there is something worrying about how quickly and confidently today's self-styled "prophets"

blame others for national disasters. Jesus tended
to discourage this presumptuous blame game
(Luke 13:2–3).

2. To say that all humans are guilty does not mean
both sides in any particular disagreement are equally
wrong. Nor does it mean all sins are equally serious.
Scripture never claims all sins are equal. In fact,
several passages seem to contradict that notion. All
sin is sin, but some sins are more damaging than
others (see Matthew 11:24; 1 Corinthians 6:18;
1 John 5:16).

3. See John M. G. Barclay, *Paul and the Gift* (Grand
Rapids: Eerdmans, 2015), 474 fn. 62.

4. See N. T. Wright, *Paul and the Faithfulness of God*, Book
Two, Parts III and IV (Minneapolis: Fortress Press,
2013), 752.

5. John Wesley put it this way, when affirming what I
have defined as "total depravity":

> Is man by nature filled with all manner of evil?
> Is he void of all good? Is he wholly fallen? Is his
> soul totally corrupted? Or, to come back to the
> text, is "every imagination of the thoughts of
> his heart evil continually?" Allow this, and you
> are so far a Christian. Deny it, and you are but a
> heathen still.

John Wesley, "Original Sin," in *Wesley's 52 Standard
Sermons* (Salem, OH: Schmul, 1988), 456. Because
of the terrible effects of sin and fallenness, Wesley
believed only grace could restore a measure of human
freedom so that we might accept or reject the free gift
of salvation in Christ.

6. Steve Jobs gave the address at the Stanford
commencement on June 12, 2005. A full

transcript can be found here: https://news.stanford
.edu/2005/06/14/jobs-061505/.

7. Walter Wink, *Unmasking the Powers: The Invisible
Forces That Determine Human Existence* (Philadelphia:
Fortress, 1986), 9 and 6, respectively.

8. "Most American Christians Do Not Believe That Satan
or the Holy Spirit Exist," Barna Group, December 11,
2015, as cited in Richard Beck, *Reviving Old Scratch:
Demons and the Devil for Doubters and the Disenchanted*
(Minneapolis: Fortress, 2016), xv.

9. Christ's supremacy over Satan and evil can be seen
in the final battle in the book of Revelation. Unlike
the final struggles in movies or books (think: *The
Lord of the Rings* or *Harry Potter*), the ultimate fight
in Revelation is over as soon as it begins. Jesus does
not duel back-and-forth with Satan and the beast and
then "win by a nose" after a closely fought contest.
Not at all. In Revelation, Christ merely shows up and
Satan is defeated (Rev. 19–20).

10. Key texts that have been seen to address Satan's fall
include Isaiah 14:12–19, Ezekiel 28, and 2 Peter 2:4.
Each of these passages is less clear in certain ways.
Still, Old Testament scholar Bruce Waltke argues
that "Satan must have rebelled against God some-
time between his creation and his encounter in the
garden." Bruce Waltke, *An Old Testament Theology: An
Exegetical, Canonical, and Thematic Approach* (Grand
Rapids: Zondervan, 2007), 273. See also Joshua
M. McNall, *The Mosaic of Atonement: An Integrated
Approach to Christ's Work* (Grand Rapids: Zondervan
Academic, 2019), chap. 9.

11. See Michael Green, *I Believe in Satan's Downfall* (Grand
Rapids: Eerdmans, 1981).

12. As reported by Eric Eyre, "Drug Firms Poured 780M Painkillers into WV Amid Rise in Overdoses," *Charleston Gazette-Mail*, December 17, 2016, www.wvgazettemail.com/news-health/20161217/drug-firms-poured-780m-painkillers-into-wv-amid-rise-of-overdoses. I encountered this story in Jake Meador, *In Search of the Common Good: Christian Fidelity in a Fractured World* (Downers Grove, IL: IVP, 2019), 44.

13. This point is made by Richard Beck, *Reviving Old Scratch: Demons and the Devil for Doubters and the Disenchanted* (Minneapolis: Fortress, 2016).

14. See James E. Tomberlin and Peter van Inwagen, eds., *Alvin Plantinga: Profiles* (Dordrect, Holland: Reidel, 1985), 43.

15. Esther Acolatse, *Powers, Principalities, and the Spirit: Biblical Realism in Africa and the West* (Grand Rapids: Eerdmans, 2018).

16. Robert Jenson, *A Theology in Outline: Can These Bones Live?* (Oxford: Oxford University Press, 2016), 60.

17. Anselm, *Cur Deus Homo*, in *Proslogium; Monologium; an Appendix in Behalf of the Fool by Gaunilon; and Cur Deus Homo?*, trans. Sidney Norton Deane (repr., Chicago: Open Court, 1926), 1.21.

18. For a balanced approach to individual and systemic sin, see Thomas H. McCall, *Against God and Nature: The Doctrine of Sin* (Wheaton, IL: Crossway, 2019), 258–70.

19. As evidence of systemic sin, Scripture has no problem claiming that corporate entities can be sinful (Rev. 2:1, 4, 12, 14–15, 18, 20; 3:1, 14–22).

20. For a painful example of social complicity in the American church, see Jemar Tisby, *The Color of Compromise: The Truth about the American*

Church's Complicity in Racism (Grand Rapids: Zondervan, 2019).

21. See T. Mark McConnell, "From 'I Have Done Wrong' to 'I Am Wrong,'" in *Locating Atonement: Explorations in Constructive Dogmatics*, eds. Oliver Crisp and Fred Sanders (Grand Rapids: Zondervan, 2015).

22. See my prior treatment of the Tamar story in Joshua M. McNall, *Perhaps: Reclaiming the Space Between Doubt and Dogmatism* (Downers Grove, IL: IVP Academic, 2021), chap. 6.

23. See Dan Lé, *The Naked Christ: An Atonement Model for a Body-Obsessed Culture* (Eugene, OR: Pickwick, 2012).

24. Philip Cunningham, *Jesus and the Evangelists* (New York: Paulist, 1988), 187.

25. A Christian writer named Jerome (AD 347–420) coined the motto: *nudus nudum Jesum sequi* ("naked to follow a naked Christ").

26. Augustine, *Homilies on the Gospel of John*, 2.2, trans. Edmund Hill (New York: New City Press, 2009), 56.

27. James K. A. Smith makes this point beautifully in *On the Road with Saint Augustine: A Real World Spirituality for Restless Hearts* (Grand Rapids: Brazos, 2019), 223.

Chapter Two: Jesus and the Severed Head

1. During Julian's lifetime, the medieval church was cracking down on the "Lollard" followers of John Wycliffe, who were condemned as heretics (in part) for writing and translating Scripture and theology in the common tongue rather than with the sanction of the church in Latin.

2. Julian wrote two works, one soon after her initial vision (*A Vision Showed to a Devout Woman*) and a much longer text (*A Revelation of Love*) which was

written after long years of prayerfully contemplating the original vision. When citing her writings, I draw from the recent critical edition by Nicholas Watson and Jacqueline Jenkins, eds., *The Writings of Julian of Norwich: A Vision Showed to a Devout Woman and a Revelation of Love* (University Park, PA: Pennsylvania State University Press, 2006). The earlier text I will reference as *Vision,* and the later text I will reference as *Revelation.*

3. Julian, *Revelation*, 51:47–48 (p. 275).

4. Ibid., 51:185–87 (p. 283).

5. For a fuller treatment of the strengths and weaknesses of Julian's Christian mysticism, see Joshua M. McNall, *Perhaps: Reclaiming the Space Between Doubt and Dogmatism* (Downers Grove, IL: IVP Academic), chap. 2.

6. Both the Greek and Latin words for *recapitulation* contain the word for "head" (*kephale* and *caput*).

7. The complicated options for interpreting what Paul means by "head" (*kephale*) are covered in Anthony C. Thiselton, *The First Epistle to the Corinthians: A Commentary on the Greek Text* (Grand Rapids: Eerdmans, 2000), 812–23.

8. Quotations cited from Walter Isaacson, *Steve Jobs* (New York: Simon & Schuster, 2011), 257.

9. In Genesis, God makes clear that Adam and Eve were not created immortal. It is the tree of life (and their ability to continue eating from it) that makes it a possibility for them to "live forever" (Gen. 3:22).

10. See Joshua M. McNall, *The Mosaic of Atonement: An Integrated Approach to Christ's Work* (Grand Rapids: Zondervan Academic, 2019), 78–79.

11. Irenaeus, *Demonstration of Apostolic Preaching*, trans. Armitage Robinson (New York: MacMillan, 1920), 22.

12. Nichole Nordeman, *Love Story: The Hand That Holds Us from the Garden to the Gate* (Brentwood, TN: Worthy Publishing, 2012), 50.

13. Colin E. Gunton, "Trinity, Ontology and Anthropology: Towards a Renewal of the Doctrine of the *Imago Dei*," in *Persons, Divine and Human: King's College Essays in Theological Anthropology*, ed. Christoph Schwöbel and Colin Gunton (London: T&T Clark, 1991), 55.

14. Tim Keller, *Making Sense of God: An Invitation to the Skeptical* (New York: Viking Penguin, 2016), 97.

15. See Mark Sayers, *Reappearing Church: The Hope for Renewal in the Rise of Our Post-Christian Culture* (Chicago: Moody Publishers, 2019), 69.

16. See Alan Noble, *You Are Not Your Own: Belonging to God in an Inhuman World* (Downers Grove, IL: IVP, 2021).

17. For all things Humboldt, see Andrea Wulf, *The Invention of Nature: Alexander von Humboldt's New World* (New York: Vintage Books, 2015).

18. Wulf, *The Invention of Nature*, 150.

19. John Muir, *My First Summer in the Sierra* (New York: Houghton Mifflin, 1911), 211.

20. Oliver D. Crisp, *Approaching the Atonement: The Reconciling Work of Christ* (Downers Grove, IL: IVP Academic, 2020), 167–68.

Chapter Three: Jesus and the Judged Judge

1. The word for justice here is rendered "righteousness" in the NIV, but the two terms are closely related.

2. Karl Barth, the great Swiss theologian, famously spoke of Jesus as "The Judge Judged in Our Place." See *Church Dogmatics*, Vol. IV, Part 1, The Doctrine of Reconciliation, trans. G. W. Bromiley; eds. Geoffrey

W. Bromiley and Thomas F. Torrance (Peabody, MA: Hendrickson, 1956/2004), § 59.2 (pp. 211–83).

3. An influential challenge to certain versions of penal substitution is by Mark Baker and Joel Green, *Recovering the Scandal of the Cross: Atonement in the New Testament and Contemporary Contexts*, 2nd ed. (Downers Grove, IL: IVP Academic, 2011).

4. A particularly un-Trinitarian version of this position is sometimes called the *Christus Odium* view of the atonement. It claims that Christ became the object of the Father's perfect hatred on the cross. This problematic understanding of the cross is found, for instance, in Wayne Grudem, *Systematic Theology* (Grand Rapids: Zondervan 1994), 575. For a critique of the *Christus Odium* position, see Joshua R. Farris and S. Mark Hamilton, "This Is My Beloved Son, Whom I Hate? A Critique of the Christus Odium Variant of Penal Substitution," in *Journal of Baptist Theological Studies* 3.2 (2018): 271–86.

5. What then should we make of Jesus's cry of "My God, my God, why have you forsaken me?" (Matt. 27:47)? Thomas McCall argues that Jesus was forsaken "unto death" (in other words, Christ was allowed to die), but not "utterly forsaken" (in other words, the Trinity was divided against itself). See Thomas McCall, *Forsaken: The Trinity and the Cross, and Why It Matters* (Downers Grove, IL: IVP Academic, 2012).

6. While those now claiming these things often hail from a segment of the Calvinist tradition, it is worth noting that John Calvin explicitly rejects this distorted view of the cross. See John Calvin, *Institutes of the Christian Religion*, trans. Henry Beveridge, Vol. 1 (Grand Rapids: Eerdmans, repr. 1981), 2.16.11.

7. In fact, many of our modern ideas about justice were derived from Scripture. C. S Lewis famously recounts how he argued against God's existence on the grounds that the universe was unjust, only to then question where he got this idea of "just" and "unjust." C. S. Lewis, *Mere Christianity* (San Francisco: Harper Collins, 2001), 38.

8. For a helpful treatment of how faith involves allegiance as well as belief, see Matthew W. Bates, *Gospel Allegiance: What Faith in Jesus Misses for Salvation in Christ* (Grand Rapids: Brazos, 2019).

9. See Jeremiah 34:18: "Those who have violated my covenant . . . I will treat like the calf they cut in two and then walked between its pieces."

10. Markus Barth, "Was Christ's Death a Sacrifice?" *Scottish Journal of Theology, Occasional Papers* 9 (Edinburgh: Oliver and Boyd, 1961), 17.

11. This refusal to describe God's form is similar to the way Isaiah describes the throne and the train of the Lord's robe, filling the temple (Isa. 6:1), but not the figure of the Lord himself.

12. For a fuller treatment of this challenging text, see Joshua M. McNall, *The Mosaic of Atonement: An Integrated Approach to Christ's Work* (Grand Rapids: Zondervan Academic, 2019), 131–34.

13. See Luke 22:37; Acts 8:32–34; 1 Peter 2:22–25.

14. See N. T. Wright, *Jesus and the Victory of God* (Minneapolis: Fortress, 1996), 602–4; also, N. T. Wright, *Justification: God's Plan and Paul's Vision* (Downers Grove, IL: IVP Academic, 2009), 226.

15. See Tony Lane, "The Wrath of God as an Aspect of the Love of God," in *Nothing Greater, Nothing Better: Theological Essays on the Love of God,* ed. Kevin J. Vanhoozer (Grand Rapids: Eerdmans, 2001), 138–67.

16. For an overview of these New Testament passages, see Michael F. Bird, *Evangelical Theology: A Biblical and Systematic Introduction*, 2nd ed. (Grand Rapids: Zondervan Academic, 2020), 642–48.

17. See Michael J. McClymond, *The Devil's Redemption: A New History and Interpretation of Christian Universalism* (Grand Rapids: Baker Academic, 2018).

18. Biblical quotations in this sentence are from John 15:5–6; Galatians 5:4; Romans 11:22; and 1 Timothy 1:19 respectively. See also Hebrews 6 and 10.

19. Jacob and Rachael Denhollander, "Justice: The Foundation of a Christian Approach to Abuse," Paper presented to the 70th Annual Meeting of the Evangelical Theological Society (Denver, CO: November 13, 2018).

20. In Trinitarian theology, this shared activity to bring about salvation involves the doctrine of "inseparable operations." The idea here is that no action of God is *ever* undertaken apart from the cooperative and harmonious interplay of Father, Son, and Spirit. To pit one member of the Trinity against another is to verge toward pagan polytheism.

21. For a treatment of how forgiveness and penalty-bearing often coexist in Scripture, see McNall, *Mosaic of Atonement*, 155–56.

22. Denhollander, "Justice," 12.

23. Ibid., 10.

24. See Rachael Denhollander, *What Is a Girl Worth?: My Story of Breaking the Silence and Exposing the Truth about Larry Nassar and USA Gymnastics* (Carol Stream, IL: Tyndale House, 2019).

25. The full transcript of Rachael Denhollander's victim impact statement (given on January 24, 2018), can be

accessed online at https://www.cnn.com/2018/01/24
/us/rachael-denhollander-full-statement/index.html.

Chapter Four: Jesus and the Double Deathblow

1. Christians as far back as John Calvin have noted
   that language of the cross sometimes functions as
   a *synecdoche*—a figure of speech (e.g., "all hands on
   deck!") in which a part is made to represent the whole.
   While synecdoche undoubtedly explains some references to the cross as good news, my argument is that
   something more is going on when biblical authors view
   Christ's death specifically as a moment of triumph.
2. N. T. Wright makes this point in numerous treatments of the resurrection. For an accessible account,
   see his *Surprised by Hope: Rethinking Heaven, the
   Resurrection, and the Mission of the Church* (New York:
   HarperOne, 2008).
3. The language of *Christus victor* and the emphasis upon
   atonement via victory was retrieved and popularized
   by Gustaf Aulén, *An Historical Study of the Three Main
   Types of the Idea of Atonement*, trans. A. G. Herbert
   (New York: MacMillen, 1960).
4. For how we are bound up "with Jesus," see chapter
   2; for a refresher on how Christ justly bears the
   penalty for human sin, see chapter 3. As we have seen
   throughout, these ideas are related in the Scriptures.
   They cannot and should not be separated.
5. Tom Holland, *Dominion: How the Christian Revolution
   Remade the World* (New York: Basic Books, 2019), 7.
6. Ibid., 2–10.
7. For more on this graffito, see my blog post, "The
   Naked God: The Cross and Body Shame," https://
   joshuamcnall.com/2016/05/11/the-naked-god-the
   -cross-and-body-shame/.

8. "Most American Christians Do Not Believe that Satan or the Holy Spirit Exist," Barna Group, Research released on April 13, 2009, https://www.barna.com /research/most-american-christians-do-not-believe -that-satan-or-the-holy-spirit-exist/.

9. The Overton window refers to the range of views on a subject that are deemed "acceptable" by a given culture at a given time.

10. See Joshua M. Moritz, "Are Viruses Evil?" in *Theology and Science* 18:4 (2020): 572 and 567 respectively.

11. See Walter Wink, *Unmasking the Powers: The Invisible Forces That Determine Human Existence* (Philadelphia: Fortress, 1986), 25–26.

12. See Isaiah 14:12–15 and Ezekiel 28:13–19.

13. Joshua M. McNall, *The Mosaic of Atonement: An Integrated Approach to Christ's Work* (Grand Rapids: Zondervan Academic, 2019), 226.

14. Satan's possession of oppressive political regimes and financial systems is especially apparent in the book of Revelation 18:3, 11–13. Here Babylon the Great is associated with the satanic dragon and his beasts. Then even after Babylon's demise, she remains a haunt for every impure spirit.

15. For a classic academic statement on the irrationality of evil, see T. F. Torrance, *Incarnation: The Person and Life of Christ*, ed. Robert T. Walker (Downers Grove, IL: IVP Academic, 2008), 244.

16. Julian, *Revelation of Love*, in *The Writings of Julian of Norwich: A Vision Showed to a Devout Woman and a Revelation of Love*, ed. Nicholas Watson and Jacqueline Jenkins (University Park, PA: Pennsylvania State University Press, 2006), 13:3–4 (p. 169).

17. Revelation 20:2 tells us explicitly that the "ancient serpent" of Genesis 3 is in fact "the devil, or Satan."

18. Jeremy R. Treat, *The Crucified King: Atonement and Kingdom in Biblical and Systematic Theology* (Grand Rapids: Zondervan Academic, 2014), 166.

19. Donald MacLeod, *Christ Crucified: Understanding the Atonement* (Downers Grove, IL: IVP Academic, 2014), 246.

20. See Leviticus 26 and Deuteronomy 28–31.

21. A classic episode of *The Simpsons* featured a grandpa who proclaims: "I'm an old man. I hate everything but *Matlock*." (This is my favorite academic endnote.)

22. See McNall, *Mosaic of Atonement*, 183.

23. Jeremy R. Treat, "Exaltation in and through Humiliation: Rethinking the States of Christ," in *Christology Ancient and Modern: Explorations in Constructive Dogmatics* (Grand Rapids: Zondervan, 2013), 114.

24. This point is made by N. T. Wright, *How God Became King: The Forgotten Story of the Gospels* (New York: HarperOne, 2012).

25. The highly symbolic book of Revelation refers to two beasts which are variously interpreted, but most scholars agree that at least part of their purpose is to show how Satan (the dragon) has co-opted the might and idolatry of Rome (including the worship of Caesar) to wage war on God's people. Following scholars like G. K. Beale, I take the expulsion of Satan from heaven (in Rev. 12:8–9) to refer not to something prior to human history, but to the result of Christ's work in the incarnation and atonement. See G. K. Beale, *The Book of Revelation: A Commentary on the Greek Text*, NIGTC (Grand Rapids: Eerdmans, 1999), 650–52.

26. For the link between Jewish ritual impurity and the forces of death, see Matthew Thiessen, *Jesus and the*

Forces of Death: The Gospels' Portrayal of Ritual Impurity within First-Century Judaism (Grand Rapids: Baker Academic, 2020).

27. In fact, David was forbidden from building God's house because of his wanton bloodshed (1 Chron. 28:3).

28. David feigned insanity to keep from being killed by the Philistines when he was on the run from Saul (1 Sam. 21:13); Jesus was thought to be insane by his own family because of the claims that he was making about God's kingdom coming through his ministry (Mark 3:21).

29. For the important place of David's suffering and his psalms of lament in highlighting Jesus as the Davidic Messiah throughout the New Testament, see Joshua W. Jipp, *The Messianic Theology of the New Testament* (Grand Rapids: Eerdmans, 2020).

Chapter Five: Jesus and Severus Snape

1. J. K. Rowling, *Harry Potter and the Deathly Hallows* (New York: Scholastic, 2007), 758.

2. See Augustine, *Confessions,* trans. Henry Chadwick (Oxford: Oxford University Press, 1991), 13.9.10 (p. 278).

3. See G. K. Beale, *We Become What We Worship: A Biblical Theology of Idolatry* (Downers Grove, IL: IVP Academic, 2008).

4. James K. A. Smith, *You Are What You Love: The Spiritual Power of Habit* (Grand Rapids: Brazos, 2016). The phrases comprise not only part of the title for Smith's work, but headings in his table of contents.

5. To be clear, Abelard did not become a monk until after his castration—which seems about right.

6. For a biographical sketch of Abelard, see Jeffrey
E. Brower and Kevin Guilfoy, eds., *The Cambridge
Companion to Abelard* (Cambridge: Cambridge
University Press, 2004), especially the introduction by
Brower and Guilfoy.

7. See Peter Abelard, *Commentary on the Epistle to the
Romans*, trans. Stephen Cartwright (Washington, DC:
Catholic University Press, 2011), 167–68.

8. Augustine, *On the Instruction of Beginners*, 4.

9. Bernard himself did not refer to Abelard's theory as
the "good example" view of the atonement. This label is
merely my attempt to simplify the essence of his case.

10. Bernard of Clairvaux, *Tractatus ad Innocentium II
Pontificem contra quaedam capitula errorum Abaelardi*,
quoted in Philip L. Quinn, "Abelard on Atonement:
'Nothing Unintelligible, Arbitrary, Illogical, or
Immoral about It,'" in *Reasoned Faith: Essays in
Philosophical Theology in Honor of Norman Kretzmann*,
ed. Eleonore Stump (Ithaca, NY: Cornell University
Press, 1993), 292.

11. Tony Jones refers to exemplarism as the "magnet"
view of atonement. See Jones, *Did God Kill Jesus?
Searching for Love in History's Most Famous Execution*
(New York: HarperOne, 2015), 154.

12. See James Denney, *The Death of Christ*, ed. R. V. G.
Tasker (1903; repr., London: Tyndale, 1951), 177.

13. Denney cites this same text at the end of his illustration in *The Death of Christ*, 177.

14. For further support, see Joshua M. McNall, *The Mosaic
of Atonement: An Integrated Approach to Christ's Work*
(Grand Rapids: Zondervan Academic, 2019), 185–87.

15. This is, of course, a scandal, and I have written many
think pieces on it.

16. In the Greek translation of Genesis 3:15, "heel" (*pterna*) is in the singular, whereas the "feet" (*podas*) in Romans 16:20 are plural.

17. See Acts 9:4, where Jesus asks: "Saul, Saul, why do you persecute me?"

18. G. B. Caird, *Principalities and Powers* (Oxford: Oxford University Press, 1956), 97.

19. Christians have historically referred to this belief as the doctrine of inseparable operations. That means that everything the triune God does outside of himself (e.g., within history) is the shared work of all three members of the Trinity. From creation to redemption, when one person of the godhead acts, all three are acting together. This belief is expressed in a famous Latin dictum (or at least . . . as famous as any Latin dictum can be these days): *Opera Trinitatis ad extra indivisa sunt* ("The outward acts of the Trinity are undivided").

20. To repeat what was said about the Father and the Son in chapter 3, Jesus willingly bears the just judgment for human sin. But the Father loves the Son perfectly and eternally, even at the crucifixion. Thus, there is no divine child abuse within atonement doctrine, or anywhere else.

21. Thanks to John Drury for making this point in a conversation over my earlier work on atonement.

22. See Alan Noble, *You Are Not Your Own: Belonging to God in an Inhuman World* (Downers Grove, IL: IVP, 2021).

23. Take, for instance, this line from Brené Brown, a teacher I enjoy, and from whom I have learned many helpful truths: "True belonging is the spiritual practice of believing in and belonging to yourself so deeply that you can share your most authentic self with the world

and find sacredness in both being part of something and standing alone in the wilderness." *Braving the Wilderness: The Quest for True Belonging and the Courage to Stand Alone* (New York: Random House, 2019), 40.

24. As some readers will recognize, "Self authoring" is the name of a self-improvement program by the psychologist and cultural guru, Jordan B. Peterson. For an introduction, see Jordan B. Peterson, "Intro to Self Authoring," August 25, 2015, YouTube video, https://www.youtube.com/watch?v=qa9u5t3C0AI. My claim in citing this example is not that there is nothing of great value in this program; I suspect there are many exercises in the "self authoring" program that are very helpful. The problem resides in the language that we can, in fact, author a new life for ourselves. For some context and critique, see Noble, *You Are Not Your Own*, 81–82.

25. See Noble, *You Are Not Your Own*.

26. This is often called the doctrine of prevenient grace, but I prefer to speak of the prevenient work of the Spirit. This doctrine means that while humans are entirely incapable of turning to God on our own, the Spirit is at work in us even before conversion to restore a measure of free will so that we may either accept or reject God's offer of new life. As such, the Spirit's prevenient work establishes a middle position between divine determinism, whereby God directly causes all our actions, both good and bad (!), and a naïve belief in human potential whereby we possess an innately free will that is capable of turning to God on our own. This middle position is sorely needed if we are to maintain that God is not the Author of evil, and humans are not the authors of our own salvation. See McNall, *Mosaic of Atonement*, 300–305.

27. West's spoken remark is frequently quoted, but I have yet to find it in any of his published works.

28. See Ephraim Radner, "Running Away from Sorrow: Pneumatology and Some Modern Discontents" in *The Third Person of the Trinity: Explorations in Constructive Dogmatics*, eds. Oliver D. Crisp and Fred Sanders (Grand Rapids: Zondervan Academic, 2020), chap. 12.

29. Rowling, *Deathly Hallows*, 662.

30. Though the Gospels spend significant time on the passion narratives themselves, the act of crucifixion itself is often described with brevity and reserve. See especially Mark's account. What's more, it wasn't that the Gospel writers lacked literary models for gorefests. Homer's *Iliad* has many R-rated accounts of killings. By avoiding this type of narrative, the Gospel writers give us cues on how we ourselves should preach the cross.

Conclusion: Universal Donor

1. To recall, *recapitulation*, in both its Greek and Latin forms, involves a reference to the "head" (*caput* in Latin, or *kephale* in Greek). Hence, I suggested that a helpful way of remembering the meaning of reca-pitulation is to view it as the "re-headshipping" of the cosmos and of the human family under Jesus, the true Human.

2. See James K. A. Smith, *You Are What You Love: The Spiritual Power of Habit* (Grand Rapids: Brazos, 2016).

Acknowledgments

Books are like babies in at least some ways. They come into the world with a mix of joy and struggle—and each one carries the DNA of more than just one person. My biggest debt of gratitude (as with our actual babies) goes to my wife, Brianna. She is my better in every way. Thanks to the Seedbed team for sowing this project, like so many others, for the church and the awakening. Thanks to Jerome Van Kuiken for providing stellar feedback all along the way. Thanks to my first group of Oklahoma Wesleyan University honors students for offering insights during our weekly tutorials. And thanks to Zondervan for believing the book was worthy of a broader audience. I pray that ordinary Christians find it to be a treatment of Christ's saving work that is written for them—since atonement doctrine isn't just for academics like myself.

The book is dedicated to my eldest son, Ewan Gregory McNall. Every day I'm grateful that I get to be his dad.